Recipes
from the Wineries
OF THE GREAT LAKES

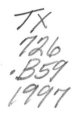

Designed by Marilyn Appleby Design
Illustrations by Pat Clubine
Edited by Ruth A. Moen

Published by Spradlin & Associates,
PO Box 863, Lapeer, MI 48446. Telephone (810) 664-8406.
First Edition.

■

RAPTOR PRESS

Raptor Press is an imprint of Spradlin & Associates.

RECIPES
FROM
THE
WINERIES
OF THE GREAT LAKES

■

JOE BORRELLO

Acknowledgments

Recipes from the Wineries of the Great Lakes is a project that was developed from the suggestions of readers and booksellers of my first book, *Wineries of the Great Lakes: A Guidebook*. It was my observation that at the wineries around the lakes, evidence of "good eating" was always present. Since my initial contact with the Great Lakes wineries had already been established, it only seemed natural that this book should come about.

It should be recognized by readers of this book that the winery families of the Great Lakes are first and foremost agricultural people. They live off the land. Their livelihood is dependent on grapes that are used in the making of juice and wine. Like other farm products, they consider grapes and wine a food and use it accordingly in their kitchens and on their dining tables.

Wine combined with food is a long-standing tradition brought over by early settlers and without the cooperation of the present generation of these farmers, craftsmen and excellent cooks, this book would not have been possible.

The author is also indebted to Chef Robert Garlough, author of *Cooking Around the Great Lakes* and director of the Grand Rapids Community College Hospitality Education Department in Michigan. His assistance in reviewing recipes and supplying insight was invaluable. Master Pastry Chef Gilles Renusson, of the same culinary program, was also helpful in testing and offering suggestions for some of the recipes.

If you have questions regarding any of the recipes, you will find it easy to contact the wineries directly. A list of the contributing wineries, their addresses and phone numbers is located in the back of the book. For further information on the Great Lakes winery region and for additional recipes, contact the following:

The Indiana Wine Grape Council
Building 20, Ste 2004
5610 Crawfordsville Road
Indianapolis, IN 46224
(317) 481-0222 or 1-800-832-WINE

The Michigan Grape and Wine Industry Council
P.O. Box 30017
Lansing, MI 48909
(517) 373-1104

New York Wine & Grape Foundation
350 Elm Street
Penn Yan, NY 14527
(315) 536-7442

Ohio Wine Producers Association
P.O. Box 157
822 N. Tote Road
Austinburg, OH 44010
(216) 466-4417

The Wine Council of Ontario
110 Hannover Dr., Ste B205
St. Catharines, Ontario, Canada L2W 1A4
(905) 684-8070

Contents

Introduction

Agriculture has always played a major role in the development of the Great Lakes Region. The abundance of water, fertile soil and the temperate climate of this glacier-carved land has long been a beacon to European settlers looking for the opportunity to improve their lives. Settlers from Germany, England, Ireland and the Netherlands came to the area and developed prosperous farms and orchards. Later, French and Italian immigrants also tilled the soil, bringing with them a passion for the grapevine. Even today, the area's wine region is highly influenced by early German, French and Italian farmers and winemakers.

The food of this area is also a reflection of this European "melting pot" ranging from hearty, basic fare to elegant cuisine designed to attract the palate and stimulate the taste buds. As Robert Garlough states in his book, *Cooking Around the Great Lakes*, "It was not long after the first settlers from the East arrived that they were joined [in the Great Lakes region] by French, Dutch, German and Scandinavian immigrants during the early and mid 1800's. They were later united with additional immigrant settlers from countries such as Italy, Poland, Russia, Czechoslovakia and Greece. Supported by the area's fertile lands, teeming lakes, abundant wild game and extensive plant life, the Native Americans and Old World brewers, bakers, farmers and dairymen joined to create the foundation of North America's heartiest regional cuisine."

The early farmers, transplanted from Europe, were well aware of the importance of wine in their daily diet. They knew from generations of experience that wine is a beverage that offers a complete range of components which tantalizes the taste buds with sweetness, acidity, saltiness and bitterness to balance these same flavor elements in food. From their kitchens they discovered that wine supplied aroma, acidity and smoothness to foods that lack those qualities. They also knew that wine accentuated food flavors. And they were not sure why, but they knew they were healthier when they consumed wine in a responsible manner with their meals.

Today, gourmets and authors of cookbooks praise wine, when used in moderation, as an inseparable companion to fine food and an indispensable ingredient in fine cookery. Often, the secret of a famous chef's recipe is the use of wine as a seasoning.

This book contains recipes that have been gathered from nearly fifty wineries in the states surrounding the Great Lakes region (Northern Indiana and Ohio, the Finger Lakes of New York, Michigan, Ontario, Northwest Pennsylvania and the Door Peninsula of Wisconsin). It incorporates the ethnic food and agricultural experiences of the individual families that make up most of the area's wine industry. Some of the recipes are quite basic at first glance, but with an added touch of regional creativity they offer intriguing subtle flavors to standard dishes. Beyond the use of wine in the Great Lakes recipes, the unusual use of seasonings, different cooking techniques and food pairings will encourage the reader to try some interesting new cooking ideas. Most all the recipes utilize the bountiful agriculture of the area, along with the use of wine as an ingredient, to present a unique brand of cuisine.

One of the most intimidating factors in cooking with wine is "which wine goes with what food." Serving wine with food is frustrating to many. If there is such a thing as a secret to matching wine with food, either in the kitchen or at the dining table, it is in selecting combinations where flavors can interact and not overpower each other. Experimentation is the best approach and don't be concerned by the use of alcohol in recipes. Alcohol boils and evaporates at 172° F. which is the temperature that water only simmers.

Then, when to use wine? If the recipe calls for water, think of using wine for at least part of the liquid required. Wine is the best liquid substitute to use for basting, braising, deglazing, marinating, poaching, sautéing, steaming and stewing. Wine is also the perfect addition to barbecue sauces, bisques, chowders, cream sauces, salad dressings, soups and stocks. In addition to its aroma and flavor, wine adds nutritionally valuable minerals and vitamins.

At this point, allow me to present only one firm rule in cooking with wine. "If it isn't good enough to drink, it isn't good enough to cook with." This does not mean, however, that you must use your best wine. A well-made and inexpensive wine is just fine and the Great Lakes has many to offer. With meats, use full-bodied dry, red wines. Fish, chicken and lighter foods are enhanced by semi-sweet or dry white wines. A nice touch to a bowl of hot broth is a tablespoon of dry sherry. For a really special treat, sparkling wines added to light cream sauces are sure to please. Avoid using so-called "cooking wines." They are usually inferior wines that contain an abundance of added salt and often impart an undesirable acidic flavor to the dish.

Wine is an agricultural product that has been placed on dining tables for centuries as a natural beverage that serves as a pleasing and sensible companion to food. It is not manufactured, nor created by man. Winemakers only guide the natural process of grape fermentation and artfully refine its subtle tastes. In cooking, wine is united with other agricultural commodities as an important flavor ingredient.

Enjoy in good health, the bounty of Mother Nature and her cornucopia of food and wine from the Great Lakes region.

God loves fermentation
just as dearly as he loves vegetation.

— *Ralph Waldo Emerson*

Frequently Asked Questions about Wine with Food

Q: I've recently increased my use of wine with cooking. Do you have any tips on cooking with wine that may be useful?

A: It seems that Americans have discovered only recently the joy of cooking with wine and the difference it can make in a very wide variety of foods. Many people have not tried cooking with wine because they are unsure of its use as a seasoning agent and how much is enough. It is difficult to overdo wine - the more you add, the more flavor you'll achieve. It all depends upon how juicy or liquid you want the finished dish. Using wine as a substitute for a portion of liquid in almost any recipe will add enormously to the flavor and richness of the dish. Experiment with a small amount of wine, so the flavors will blend subtly and not become overpowering. Wine gives flavor to some dishes that would be bland or flat without it. The flavor of wine in cooking is due to the nature of the wine and not the alcohol. During cooking, most of the alcohol evaporates (alcohol boils and evaporates at 172 degrees F., the temperature at which water only simmers) and little alcohol is present in the finished dish. For meat dishes calling for wine, first heat the wine (do not boil or you will lose the flavor). Adding cold wine tends to make meat tough, while warm wine helps tenderize it. For fish and chicken, use a dry or semi-dry white wine. Dry red wines have a better chemistry with heavier red meats. One thing to keep in mind is that when wine is first added to a dish it imparts little flavor. Therefore, it is best to let it cook for a few minutes before tasting. You will be astonished at the difference even 5 minutes makes.

Q: Is there any special type of wine to use for cooking?

A: Not the one that is labeled "Cooking Wine." Rule Number One: "If it isn't good enough to drink, it isn't good enough to cook with." So-called "Cooking Wine" usually has a lot of sodium added. This does not mean, however, that you should use your best wine. A well-made and inexpensive jug wine is just fine.

Q: Which wines are proper with which foods?

A: The word "proper" creates a misconception about wine for many people. If you like the wine, it's proper. There are no laws that must be obeyed. Having said that, however, sweet wines have a tendency to numb the tastes buds, so keep that in mind when you are trying to match food with wine. Dry or semi-dry wines would be preferable with meals. Generally speaking, this will allow you to maximize the pleasure of both the wine and the flavor of the food. Experiment on your own with different foods and sauces, you'll be amazed at the different taste sensations that can be created by changing the wine companion.

Q: I've always used the guideline of "white wine with white meat and red wine with red meat." Does this still apply?

A: It's still a pretty good rule of thumb, but today's cooking is much more sophisticated and complex. Many of the old cooking "laws" are being thrown out the window by enterprising young chefs who are constantly looking for new and different approaches to making food more interesting. Today, fish and chicken dishes are being served with red sauces and beef with cream and herb sauces. Now, what wine do we serve? The key is to try different combinations of food and wine. There really is no set rule and it is quite acceptable to have a light red wine with a spicy Cajun seafood dish or a hearty white wine with a beef entree. There are still flavor combinations of food that are more naturally complemented by certain wines, but the main objective is to enjoy what you are eating and the wine you are drinking. Experiment and let your palate be your guide.

Q: Would you recommend using champagne in cooking?

A: The high acid content of sparkling wines and their bubbles add a real tantalizing tanginess to light cream sauces. While champagne-style wines are generally considered festive beverages only, they are also excellent wines for cooking delicate sauce dishes. It may seem a bit extravagant to cook with champagne, but use only about half as much "bubbly" as you would a still table wine, due to the higher acidity. Sparkling wines will add a little zest to your recipes, but they will retain the bubbles for only a short time. You would be better served if you put it in your sauce just before serving the dish.

Q: What does wine add to a sauce and how do I use it?

A: Wine is a seasoning like herbs or spices, only in liquid form. It accents and improves natural food flavors. It also adds a certain flair to ordinary cooking; and yet, it is easy to use. Instead of adding water, which is tasteless, to your recipe, substitute some wine. You'll discover a much more fragrant and better-tasting dish. Add the wine near the end of your cooking for more intense flavoring.

Q: *Does wine make a good marinade?*

A: Meat may be tenderized and its flavor enhanced by marinating in red wine for an hour or two. You'll also find adding white wine to a seafood marinade will break down the odorous fish oils, just as lemon juice and vinegar do. Marinating should be done in glass, porcelain or materials other than aluminum, which has a tendency to give an off-flavor to a wine marinade. Some of the Great Lakes semi-sweet wines and champagnes are particularly pleasing as a marinade for fresh fruit served in a wine glass, plus they add an elegant touch to your table setting.

Q: *What wines would you suggest with appetizers before a dinner party?*

A: Appetizers and aperitif wines are meant to tease and stimulate the palate before a meal. They should be dry or off-dry. Sweet wines have a tendency to numb the taste buds and overpower food flavors. Light bodied, semi-dry white wines like Riesling, Vidal Blanc and some of the new "proprietary" wines have refreshing tastes and sensations that make them easy to sip before dinner. They are especially appealing to guests who don't normally drink wine and are appreciated by those who have cut back on the consumption of hard liquor. The slight residual sugar in these wines will go well with appetizers that are smoked, salty or spiced. Dry sparkling and still white wines tend to cleanse and sharpen one's palate. Seyval, Chardonnay, Sauvignon Blanc and Vignoles serve very well with the delicate flavors of a wide variety of shellfish and seafood hors d'oeuvres. A combination of complementing flavors have a tendency to stimulate your guests' appetites.

Q: *What wine would you recommend serving with rack of lamb?*

A: The classic wine would be Cabernet Sauvignon or Merlot, but Zinfandel and Chancellor could be just as pleasing. The reason these wines marry so well with lamb is because the meat's slight oiliness softens the wine tannin and enables the wine's subtler flavors to develop and stand out.

Q: *What wines are best with game birds?*

A: Quail and game hens have a sweet meat that affects other flavors. For example, grilled quail with herbs will have a smoky character that would be compatible with a dry Sauvignon Blanc, Seyval or Chardonel. The same bird roasted and served with a wine sauce might better match a Pinot Noir or Chancellor. Squab, a dark meat, stronger-flavored bird, usually needs a fruity, acidic red or white wine that can handle the distinctive gamey taste. Marinating any of these birds in a Great Lakes fruit or berry wine presents a fruitier flavor that would be delicious with a Pinot Noir or young Foch. Selecting a wine, however, will be influenced by the cooking method, sauces, stuffings and marinades that are used with any of these dishes.

Q: Is it me or does wine not go very well with the salad course? I seem to have a real hard time enjoying wine with salads containing vinaigrette dressings. Are there other foods that may also not be compatible with wine?

A: Although drinking wine with a vinaigrette salad dressing may be undesirable, many cooks prefer vinegar made of wine. Strange as it may sound, wine vinegar does have a decidedly less harsh taste than cider varieties. Thus, it intermingles with and adds complexity rather than dominating other food flavors and smells. Wine vinegars can be found as red, white, herbed and spiced. They add a nice touch to a tasty crisp salad. Most foods go well with wine, but there are some flavors which should be worked around or toned down when wine is an important part of the meal. Included in these are curry, horseradish, hot peppers, citrus rinds, excessive fats and oils and heavy chocolate. In addition, one surprising food is asparagus. It can dull your palate, so it is better served as a separate course without wine.

Q: Could you make some suggestions about which wines to serve with cheese?

A: Flavored cream cheeses match well with Great Lakes fruit wines. Chardonnay is a hit with almost any mild, soft cheese offered as an appetizer. White Cheddar and Merlot are natural partners, as are Brie and Pinot Gris. Try Marechal Foch or Chambourcin with the popular goat cheeses and Chancellor or Cabernet Sauvignon with fresh Parmesan or Asiago. How about pairing a blue cheese with either Cream Sherry or a Great Lakes Late Harvest Riesling for dessert? Of course, port and aged cheddar or Stilton are classic matches. You should have no problem finding either the cheeses or the wines at the specialty food and wine section of the supermarket. Wine and cheese are natural food partners and have a lot in common. Both are products of the fermentation process and offer a wide variety of styles from simple and mild to complex and aged. "Wine and cheese" is one of the most popular and appealing party themes for contemporary entertaining.

Q: What is the classic food match-up with champagne?

A: Although a lot of a people would like to believe that a "touch of the bubbly" complements most any meal or course, I have found that sparkling wines always are at their finest as the aperitif with hors d'oeuvres and then again with dessert. In my opinion, the bubbles distract the taste buds from the more complex flavors of a main entree. An exception to this would be "brunch" where champagne does seem to have a very complementary effect on the combination of foods and it does add to an atmosphere of "casual decadence".

Q: How do I go about putting together a wine-tasting party for friends?

A: Organizing a wine-tasting is relatively simple and offers a unique experience for your guests. The first thing you have to determine is the theme. For instance, "The Wines of the Niagara Peninsula" or "Champagnes of the Great Lakes." The possibilities are endless and your local wine merchant will be of invaluable help in the planning. Always plan a selection of different styles of wines and serve the whites before the reds and the dry before the sweet wines. This will make it easier for your taste buds to distinguish subtle differences. Have plenty of food snacks available, but stay away from heavily seasoned or flavored foods that may overpower the wines. For those who may wish to know more about the wines, many trade associations and wineries offer booklets and materials, usually free for the asking. Be sure to have non-alcoholic drinks, such as sparkling juices for the designated drivers and plan about a total of twelve to fourteen ounces per person for the evening.

Q: How much wine should I plan to serve for dinner quests?

A: That question is always a bit difficult to answer because there are variables. There are approximately six, four-ounce servings in a normal .750 ml wine bottle. At a quick luncheon, one glass a person might be enough, but at a long dinner, five or six might not be too much. A total of half a bottle per person (combining different wines) is a reasonable average allowance for most people and occasions. But the circumstance and mood of the meal, and above all how long it goes on, are the deciding factors. There is a golden rule for hosts, be generous, but never pressing.

Q: At a wine tasting party, in what order should red, white and sparkling wines be served? Do "blush" wines follow the reds?

A: As a general rule, serve white wines before reds and dry wines before sweet. Blush wines are served as you would rosé, in between the white and the red wines. The serving order is a matter of common sense rather than one of etiquette. Sweet wines have a tendency to overpower the taste buds which will give the sensation of bitterness to dry wines after the palate has been stimulated with sweetness. Heartier red wines have the same effect over white wines, so it only makes sense to serve in the suggested order to get the most enjoyment from the wines. Sparkling wines with their higher acid content and bubbles, have a tendency to clear and cleanse the palate so they may be served first or last with no loss in taste.

Q: Are fruit wines better by themselves than at the dinner table?

A: Great Lakes fruit wines make refreshing cocktails, punches and aperitifs when mixed with sparkling soda, white wine or on ice. As far as with food, fruit wine is an excellent ingredient for cooking. They enrich sauces, desserts and nothing is more tasty than a turkey, chicken or ham that is basted with a peach, cherry or raspberry wine. When using fruit wines for basting or sauces, serve a medium-dry white or sparkling wine with the dish. For desserts, try Great Lakes fruit wines over a bowl of fresh fruit or in your special mousse recipe. There are dozens of dessert recipes, from cakes to ice cream, that explode with flavor when fruit wines are added.

Q: What is the proper procedure for setting wine glasses at the dinner table?

A: It is preferable to have a fresh, clean glass for each wine planned with a meal. The glasses should be clear stemware and capable of holding eight to ten ounces of wine. Etiquette dictates placing the wine glasses in the upper right-hand portion of the place setting. The wines are poured half to two thirds full, from the first glass on the right of each guest (for the first course) to the last glass on the left (for dessert). If you do not have enough glasses for all the wines, use what you have and supply a pitcher of fresh water to rinse after each wine. There are some traditional wine glass shapes from various wine regions, but the all-purpose, 8 to 10 ounce, tulip-shaped glass works very well for all types of wines.

Q: I received a hostess gift of wine from my dinner guests, but it didn't match with the menu I had planned. Did I make a social blunder by not opening and serving the wine my friends brought?

A: The thoughtful gift was exactly that and is meant to be enjoyed by you at your leisure as a token of appreciation. If your friends expected to share the wine with you they should have told you ahead of time that they would like to bring the wine and asked for your recommendation to complement the menu.

Q: How do I keep wine left over from dinner from going bad?

A: Once wine has been exposed to oxygen outside of the bottle it begins to deteriorate. If you were to recork the bottle and place it in the refrigerator, it should delay the deterioration process for a few days. It will be drinkable, but not exactly as it was originally at the dinner table. If you purchase large containers and decant them into smaller air-tight bottles, the wine should be suitable for leisurely serving later without losing much quality. There are also a number of reliable products on the market like "Vacu Vin" that remove the oxygen in the bottle or replace it with nitrogen for temporary storage.

Q: A friend served me a sweet dessert wine he called "Ice Wine". Can you tell me a little about it?

A: What your friend served you was a Great Lakes style of sweet wine called "Icewine" because of harvest conditions. The grapes are left ripening on the vine well into the winter season when they may be subject to a hard freeze. Since it is the water content of the grapes that freezes, the juice is a mixture of concentrated sugar, acidity and other flavor components. The grapes are gathered during the evening and early morning while they are still frozen and pressed immediately to separate the juice concentrate from the ice. After fermentation, the resulting wine is quite sweet with the capacity for a very long life. The Germans originated *Eiswein* and it is almost an accident of nature and not available in every harvest. Niagara-on-the Lake, Ontario and New York's Finger Lakes produce some of the best "Ice Wine" in the world on a consistent basis.

Q: My doctor said a little wine at dinner helps digest my food. Why so?

A: According to some medical practitioners, the acidity in wine helps break down protein in the digestive process. As we pass the age of 50, it seems our system does not produce as much hydrochloric acid to aid digestion and hence, many doctors are suggesting a glass or two of wine with a meal. Wine also has a tranquil effect on the body and aids some people who have trouble sleeping. As St. Paul, the Apostle, said in 1 Timothy 5:23, "Drink no longer water, but use a little wine for thy stomach's sake." As in all consumption and responsible use of alcoholic beverages, moderation is the key to safe and healthful enjoyment.

Appetizers

Cheddar Wine Straws

From McGregor Vineyard, Finger Lakes, New York

Serves 10

1 cup butter
2 cups sharp cheddar cheese, grated
2 2/3 cups flour
1/4 teaspoon salt
 dash red pepper
4 tablespoons dry white wine

A popular "munchy" with a glass of McGregor Chardonnay.

Mix like pie crust, cutting butter into flour, add cheese. Gradually add wine until it holds together. Chill. Roll on lightly floured board and cut in narrow strips with pastry wheel or knife. Place on ungreased sheets. Bake 350 degrees F. for 30-40 minutes or until crisp and very light brown.

Per serving: 377 Calories; 26g Fat (63% calories from fat); 9g Protein; 26g Carbohydrate; 73mg Cholesterol; 380mg Sodium

NOTES

Cheesy Wine Mold

From McGregor Vineyard, Finger Lakes, New York

Serves 8

10 ounces sharp cheddar cheese,
  shredded
1/8 teaspoon nutmeg
1/8 teaspoon white pepper
1/4 cup Riesling wine
4 tablespoons butter

Serve with apple and pear wedges along with McGregor Riesling.

Combine cheese, butter, nutmeg and pepper. Heat wine to boiling, immediately pour over cheese. Beat with electric mixer until smooth, about 10 minutes. Cover. Chill overnite. Unmold onto serving plate.

Cover and let stand at room temperature 1-2 hours before serving.

Per serving: 198 Calories; 17g Fat (81% calories from fat); 9g Protein; 1g Carbohydrate; 52mg Cholesterol; 278mg Sodium

NOTES

_____

_____

_____

_____

_____

_____

_____

Cherry Nut Loaf Quick Bread

From von Stiehl Winery, Wisconsin

Serves 12

2 cups all-purpose flour
2 teaspoons baking powder
2 teaspoons baking soda
3/4 teaspoon salt
1/2 cup shortening
1/2 cup sugar
2 medium eggs
1/2 cup cherries, dried
1/4 cup sweet cherry wine
1/2 cup nuts finely chopped

A perfect addition to an appetizer buffet or for dessert with a chilled glass of von Stiehl Sweet Cherry wine.

Lightly grease and flour a 9 x 5 x 3 inch pan, set aside. In a small mixing bowl stir the flour, baking powder, baking soda and salt, set aside.

In a medium bowl cream the shortening and sugar until light and fluffy. Add eggs and dry cherries. Beat well. Add cherry wine gradually. Slowly blend in flour mixture. Add nuts and beat well. Pour into pan and bake at 350 degrees F. for 45-50 minutes or until a toothpick inserted in center comes out clean. Remove from pan and turn on side on a wire rack to cool. Makes 1 loaf.

Per serving: 234 Calories; 13g Fat (49% calories from fat); 4g Protein; 26g Carbohydrate; 30mg Cholesterol; 414mg Sodium

NOTES

_____

_____

_____

_____

Country Ham Holiday Meatballs

From Chef Tom Johnson, Lonz Winery, Ohio

Makes 60

1 medium onion, finely minced
2 tablespoons canola oil
1/4 teaspoon rosemary leaves, finely chopped
1 egg lightly whisked
1 teaspoon dry mustard
1 clove garlic, finely minced
1/4 teaspoon Tabasco sauce
1/2 cup bread crumbs, finely ground
2 tart apples, cored & minced
1 pound ham, smoked & ground
1/2 pound pork, lean & ground
2 cups flour for dredging

> The perfect centerpiece for
> "al fresco" entertaining
> with Lonz Concord wine.

Cook the onions in the canola oil, with rosemary, over low heat, until they are soft and transparent. Remove from heat and reserve.

Combine the remaining ingredients, except the dredging flour, in a large mixing bowl. Add the onions and thoroughly blend all of the ingredients. Using a 2-tablespoon plastic or metal scoop (also called a cookie dropper), shape into cocktail size meatballs. Drop the scooped meatballs into the flour, or a combination of flour and some additional breadcrumbs, for dredging, smoothing up their shape as well. Place the floured balls in rows on a sided cookie sheet or jelly roll pan, lined with oiled aluminum foil. When all of the balls are formed, refrigerate them for an hour or so.

Preheat oven to 350 degrees F. Place the baking sheet on the center rack. Bake for about 30 minutes, turning once, until the meatballs are just done. Serve with our own GREAT LAKES VINEYARD BARBECUE SAUCE (see recipe) or a quality commercial Chinese Sweet-and-Sour Sauce.

Per serving: 47 Calories; 2g Fat (37% calories from fat); 3g Protein; 5g Carbohydrate; 9mg Cholesterol; 118mg Sodium

Duck Liver Pate

From Chef Erik Peacock, Henry of Pelham Winery, Ontario

Serves 4

1/4 pound duck liver, smoked optional
1/4 pound butter, room temperature
1/4 large onion, finely diced
1 clove garlic, minced
1 pinch thyme
1 pinch nutmeg
1 pinch ground cloves
1 ounce brandy
salt and pepper to taste

A delectable treat that can be made up to four days in advance and served with Henry of Pelham Cabernet/Merlot.

Melt half the butter in a saute pan. Add the onion and garlic and cook until translucent and soft.

Add the duck liver and cook completely. Add the dried spices and brandy and cook for 1-2 minutes. Cool to room temperature.

Blend in food processor with remaining half of butter until smooth and place in a crock to chill.

For an added treat serve on GREEN ONION CREPES topped with SAUTEED SLIVERS OF MUSCOVY DUCK BREAST IN A BLACK CURRANT GLAZE (see recipes).

Per serving: 261 Calories; 24g Fat (88% calories from fat); 6g Protein; 2g Carbohydrate; 208mg Cholesterol; 309mg Sodium

NOTES

_____

_____

_____

_____

_____

Garlic Spread

From Fenn Valley Vineyards, Michigan

Serves 4

1 cup garlic cloves, peeled
1 small onion, finely chopped
2 teaspoons Worcestershire sauce
1 tablespoon white wine, semi-dry
1/2 teaspoon olive oil
3/4 teaspoon thyme
1 1/2 tablespoons nonfat Parmesan cheese

A delicious start to an Italian or grilled meat menu with a glass of Fenn Valley Chancellor.

Mix all ingredients, except cheese, together in an oven-proof bowl. Cover and bake at 350 degrees F. for 1 1/2 hours or until the mixture starts to turn dark and carmelize. Do not let the onion or garlic burn.

Remove from the oven. Add 1 tablespoon of parmesan cheese. Stir in cheese while mashing the garlic. Smooth the top of the garlic paste in the bowl and sprinkle the remaining cheese on top.

Bake uncovered for 5-10 minutes or until the cheese is lightly browned.

Serve while hot. Use as a spread on toasted bread, bread sticks or crackers.

Per serving: 75 Calories; 1g Fat (9% calories from fat); 4g Protein; 14g Carbohydrate; 0mg Cholesterol; 210mg Sodium

NOTES

_____

_____

_____

_____

_____

_____

Green Onion Crepes

From Chef Erik Peacock, Henry of Pelham Winery, Ontario

Serves 4

1 cup all-purpose flour
1 tablespoon sugar
1/4 teaspoon salt
1 cup milk
1/3 cup water
3 eggs
3 tablespoons unsalted butter, melted
1/4 cup green onions, minced

Classic crepes are a base for your favorite hors d'oeuvre recipe and a glass of Henry of Pelham Winery Chardonnay or Riesling.

Combine the flour, sugar and salt in a food processor and process briefly. With the motor running, add the milk, eggs, water and butter through the feed tube and process until smooth.

Add the green onions and pulse machine once or twice to mix. Let stand in refrigerator for 1 hour.

Heat non-stick skillet until quite hot and pour in 3 tablespoons of batter and quickly tilt pan so the batter spreads evenly forming a crepe. Cook until lightly brown, about 30-45 seconds. Turn once and cook another 15 seconds.

Put wax or parchment paper between each crepe and cover stack with plastic wrap. These crepes can be made up to 2 days in advance and held in the refrigerator.

Use your favorite cream cheese, fruit or vegetable filling recipe to form roll-up appetizers or fold crepes to form rough triangles and spread each with DUCK LIVER PATE and top with sliced DUCK BREAST IN A BLACK CURRANT GLAZE (see recipes).

Per serving: 293 Calories; 15g Fat (45% calories from fat); 9g Protein; 31g Carbohydrate; 168mg Cholesterol; 207mg Sodium

NOTES

_____

_____

_____

Gruyere Stuffed Mushrooms

From McGregor Vineyard, Finger Lakes, New York

Serves 8

1 pound fresh mushroom caps
3/4 cup Gruyere cheese
1/4 cup Jarlsberg cheese
6 tablespoons dry bread crumbs
1 clove garlic, minced
2 tablespoons butter, softened
1 tablespoon Chardonnay wine
1 egg, hard-boiled

A party favorite with McGregor Chardonnay.

Combine cheese, egg, crumbs, garlic and wine. Fill mushroom caps with mixture. Melt butter and lightly coat bottom of baking pan, place mushrooms in pan, drizzle remaining butter over mushrooms and sprinkle with bread crumbs.

Bake at 375 degrees F. for 15-20 minutes. Crisp under broiler at end of baking.

Per serving: 87 Calories; 7g Fat (75% calories from fat); 4g Protein; 1g Carbohydrate; 22mg Cholesterol; 91mg Sodium

NOTES

_____

_____

_____

_____

_____

_____

_____

Morel Frittata

From L. Mawby Vineyards, Michigan

Serves 8

2 cups morels, cleaned and chopped
1 cup onion, chopped
1 tablespoon olive oil
1 teaspoon butter
6 whole eggs, slightly beaten
1 teaspoon Vegetable Magic
  (packaged seasoning mix)*
1 1/2 teaspoons Veg-It
  (packaged seasoning mix)*
1/4 cup dry white wine
1/2 teaspoon salt

A guest-pleaser as a buffet or brunch item served with L. Mawby Vignoles Sur Lie wine.

    Mix seasonings in eggs and set aside.

    Saute onions in oil and butter until transparent. Add morels and simmer until dry. Add wine and simmer until dry. Blend into egg mixture, then pour into 9" pie plate and cook in preheated oven at 350 degrees F. for about 20-30 minutes.

    *Vegetable Magic and Veg-It are commercial prepackaged seasoning mixes available in the specialty food section of grocery or gourmet stores.

Per serving: 80 Calories; 5g Fat (65% calories from fat); 5g Protein; 2g Carbohydrate; 137mg Cholesterol; 253mg Sodium

NOTES

_____

_____

_____

_____

_____

Mushroom Pastry

From McGregor Vineyard, Finger Lakes, New York

Makes 60 bite-sized appetizers

FILLING:
2 tablespoons butter
1/2 pound mushrooms, chopped
1/4 cup onion, chopped
1/2 teaspoon salt
1/2 teaspoon pepper
1 teaspoon lemon juice
2 teaspoons flour
dash nutmeg
1/2 cup sour cream
1/2 teaspoon dill weed

Tasty little morsels best served with any of McGregor Vineyard Sparkling wines.

PASTRY:
2 cups flour
8 ounces cream cheese
1/2 pound butter
2 teaspoons milk
2 egg yolks

Saute mushrooms and onion in butter and lemon juice. Add salt and pepper, flour, sour cream and dill weed and set aside.

Mix pastry ingredients (flour, cream cheese and butter) like a pie crust. Cut into 3 inch circles and add about 1 teaspoon of filling. Fold into crescents and pinch closed. Glaze with milk and egg yolk mixture.

Bake at 350 degrees F. for 25-30 minutes.

Per serving: 66 Calories; 5g Fat (72% calories from fat); 1g Protein; 4g Carbo-hydrate; 21mg Cholesterol; 68mg Sodium

NOTES

_____

_____

Pork Meatballs with Carmelized Sweet & Sour Sauce

From Lucas Vineyards, Finger Lakes, New York

Makes 40-50

2 pounds ground pork
4 tablespoons mango pickle,
  (in the mid-eastern section)
1/4 red pepper, diced
2 Roma tomatoes, peel, seed & dice
1 teaspoon ground cumin
1/4 cup seasoned bread crumbs
1/2 teaspoon ground coriander
2 tablespoons garlic pickle (Indian
  seasoning)
2 tablespoons fresh cilantro,
  chopped
3 scallions, chopped
1 clove garlic, minced
2 egg yolks

SAUCE RECIPE
1 tablespoon sesame oil
1 tablespoon corn oil

A party hit when served with Lucas Vineyards Seyval Blanc wine.

1/4 cup onion, chopped
4 cloves garlic, minced
3 slices ginger root, thinly sliced
3 star anise
1 teaspoon red pepper
1 tablespoon water
1 teaspoon cornstarch
1 teaspoon salt
1/2 cup chicken stock
1 cup sugar
1/4 cup balsamic vinegar
1/2 cup dry white wine, Seyval Blanc
1/4 cup rice vinegar
1/2 cup tomato sauce
1/2 cup soy sauce

Meatballs: Blend all ingredients, except pork, in processor. Mix with pork. Shape into balls and bake at 375 degrees F. for 20 minutes.
Sauce: Heat sesame and corn oil in skillet. Add onions, garlic, ginger root, anise & red pepper to oil and cook until onions are translucent and set aside.

Combine 2 tablespoon stock and all the sugar in heavy pan; stir constantly over med-high heat until carmelized (about 10 minutes). Add balsamic vinegar, rice vinegar and wine to caramelized sugar and stir until sugar is dissolved (5 minutes). Add soy sauce and tomato sauce to caramelized sauce. Add onion mixture and remaining stock to sauce mixture and cook for 5 minutes.

Combine cornstarch and water thoroughly and add to sauce with salt. Continue to cook over low heat until reduced by half, stirring occasionally. Strain sauce and discard solids. Will keep covered in fridge for approximately a week.

Per serving: 113 Calories; 6g Fat (47% calories from fat); 7g Protein; 8g Carbohydrate; 32mg Cholesterol; 290mg Sodium

Red Wine Jelly Dogs

From Fulkerson's Winery & Juice Plant, Finger Lakes, New York

Serves 8

1/3 cup yellow mustard
1 pound hot dogs cut cocktail size

RED WINE JELLY:
2 teaspoons lemon juice
1 cup sugar
1 cup red wine
1/4 bottle pectin

Simple and quick to disappear at a party. The Fulkerson family serves their Reserve Red with this "munchy."

For jelly, mix ingredients and bring to a boil. Continue boiling for one minute, stirring constantly.

Blend in mustard and add cut up hot dogs or cocktail franks. Serve in chaffing dish.

Per serving: 313 Calories; 17g Fat (51% calories from fat); 7g Protein; 29g Carbohydrate; 28mg Cholesterol; 766mg Sodium

NOTES

_____

_____

_____

_____

_____

_____

_____

Sauteed Mushrooms on Toasted Hearts

From Reif Estate Winery, Ontario

Serves 12

1 bunch green onions, finely chopped
3 tablespoons extra virgin olive oil
3 large tomatoes, peeled and chopped
1 teaspoon oregano
1 tablespoon balsamic vinegar
2 tablespoons parsley
2 cups fresh mushrooms, washed & sliced
1/2 cup dry white wine
salt and pepper to taste

Warm or cold, this one is a crowd pleaser when presented with a glass of Reif Estate Chardonnay.

Heat oil in skillet and add onions, saute until they have a golden color. Place tomatoes, oregano and vinegar in the skillet with the onions. Stir. Put lid on skillet and saute for 5 minutes then add mushrooms, parsley and wine and cook for 10 more minutes. Just before serving add salt and pepper to taste.

Use a heart cookie cutter to cut toast as it comes out of the toaster. Serve warm or cold on the toasted hearts.

Per serving: 51 Calories; 4g Fat (66% calories from fat); 1g Protein; 3g Carbohydrate; 0mg Cholesterol; 8mg Sodium

NOTES

_____

_____

_____

_____

_____

Sesame-Chutney Cheese Log

From Chateau Grand Traverse, Michigan

Serves 24

3 ounces cream cheese
1/4 cup rose wine, Gamay
3 tablespoons chutney, cherry
1/4 tablespoon salt
3/4 pound Monterey Jack cheese,
    grated
1/3 cup sesame seeds toasted

A tasty appetizer with your favorite crackers and a bottle of Chateau Grand Traverse Gamay Noir Rose wine.

    Beat cream cheese until soft; blend in wine, chutney, salt and grated cheese. Shape into 2-inch log, 10 inches long.
    Toast sesame seeds in 400 degrees F. oven until golden, about 5 minutes. Roll cheese log in seeds; chill until firm, about 2 hours.

Per serving: 83 Calories; 7g Fat (72% calories from fat); 4g Protein; 1g Carbohydrate; 17mg Cholesterol; 160mg Sodium

NOTES

_____

_____

_____

_____

_____

_____

_____

_____

Spaghetti Pretzels

From Lakeshore Winery, Finger Lakes, New York

Serves 20

20 ounces pretzels,
  salted or unsalted
1/2 cup vegetable oil
1 package dry spaghetti sauce
  seasoning mix
1/4 cup Parmesan cheese, grated
2 tablespoons dry red wine

This recipe gives a whole new meaning to party snacks, especially when served with Lakeshore Baco Noir. You'll never go back to plain old pretzels again.

Preheat oven to 250 degrees F. Pour the pretzels into a large bowl, pour the vegetable oil over the pretzels and stir until evenly coated. Sprinkle on the spaghetti sauce seasoning and parmesan cheese a little at a time, stirring after each addition. Add the wine and stir again. Bake in a 13-by-9 inch baking pan for 30 minutes, stirring about half way through.

Per serving: 162 Calories; 7g Fat (37% calories from fat); 3g Protein; 23g Carbohydrate; 1mg Cholesterol; 505mg Sodium

NOTES

_____

_____

_____

_____

_____

_____

_____

Vegetarian Pate

From Lakeshore Winery, Finger Lakes, New York

Serves 14

1/4 cup extra-virgin olive oil
4 cloves garlic, whole and peeled
12 ounces fresh mushrooms,
   rinsed and drained
8 leaves Italian basil, rinsed and drained
1 teaspoon salt
1 tablespoon Catawba or semi-sweet wine
plain crackers or Melba toast rounds

A tasty "munchy" for a cocktail party to complement Lakeshore Aunt Clara wine, a fruity, semi-sweet Catawba grape wine.

   Stir oil and garlic in a large skillet or wok over medium heat until garlic is soft and golden. Add mushrooms and continue stirring until mushrooms are soft, about 5 minutes.

   Put the mushrooms, oil and garlic in a blender or food processor. Add the basil, salt and wine. Process until smooth, about 30 seconds. Refrigerate and serve on plain crackers.

Per serving: 41 Calories; 4g Fat (83% calories from fat); 1g Protein; 1g Carbohydrate; 0mg Cholesterol; 153mg Sodium

NOTES

_____

_____

_____

_____

_____

_____

_____

Wine Cheese Spread

From Warner Vineyards, Michigan

Serves 8

8 ounces cream cheese
8 ounces sharp cheddar cheese,
  grated
1/4 cup blush or rose wine
1/4 teaspoon onion salt
1/4 teaspoon garlic salt
1 1/2 teaspoons onion soup mix

Nothing complicated about this appetizer spread/dip. Just serve Warner's Classic Blush and your guests will love it.

It's simple. Just mix it all together until it looks right. If you want to use it as a dip, add more wine until thin enough. For the diet conscious, substitute no-fat cream cheese and low-fat cheddar cheese.

Per serving: 216 Calories; 19g Fat (80% calories from fat); 9g Protein; 2g Carbohydrate; 61mg Cholesterol; 393mg Sodium

NOTES

_____

_____

_____

_____

_____

_____

_____

Beverages

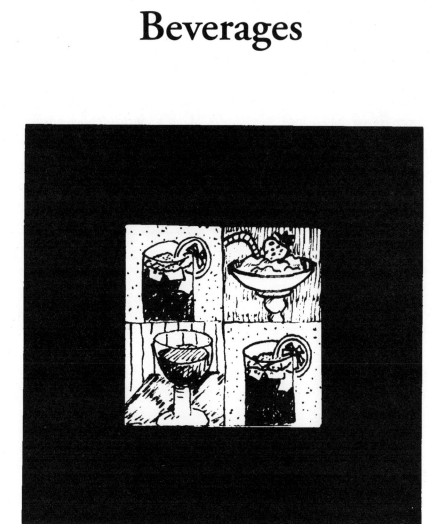

Champagne Blossom Punch

From Chateau Grand Traverse, Michigan

Serves 10

2/3 cup frozen orange juice
   concentrate, thawed
1/3 cup frozen lemonade
   concentrate, thawed
1 2/3 cups Riesling wine, chilled
1 cup water, cold
3 1/3 cups Champagne
   (one bottle)
lemon, lime or orange slices
   for garnish

Here's a festive punch adapted from Good Housekeeping Magazine with the addition of Chateau Grand Traverse Sweet Johannisberg Riesling.

In a punch bowl combine orange juice and lemonade concentrates. Add wine and water, stir to combine. Add champagne, but do not stir. If desired, float an ice ring with fruit slices on top. Serve immediately

Per serving: 124 Calories; 0g Fat (1% calories from fat); 0g Protein; 10g Carbohydrate; 0mg Cholesterol; 3mg Sodium

NOTES

_____

_____

_____

_____

_____

_____

_____

Champagne Punch

From Michigan Grape & Wine Industry Council

Serves 10

50 ounces Champagne (2 bottles)
2 liters club soda
4 ounces Curacao or Triple Sec
4 ounces brandy
4 ounces maraschino cherry juice
1/2 cup sugar, optional

A great holiday crowd pleaser with Michigan champagnes.

Mix together in punch bowl with a large block of ice. Garnish with whole cherries, strawberries, orange or lemon slices.

Per serving: 234 Calories; 0g Fat (0% calories from fat); 0g Protein; 21g Carbohydrate; 0mg Cholesterol; 48mg Sodium

NOTES

_____

_____

_____

_____

_____

_____

_____

_____

Hot Cranberry-Melba Cabernet Sauvignon

From Kittling Ridge Estate Wines & Spirits, Ontario

Serves 6

750 milliliters Cabernet Sauvignon
  (1 bottle)
8 ounces cranberry cocktail, frozen
  concentrate thawed, undiluted
1/2 cup raspberry jam
1/2 cup Pear or Framboise Eau de Vie
1 teaspoon ground cinnamon

A refreshing way to ward off the chill of winter especially with Kittling Ridge Cabernet and Stillmaster's Eau de Vie.

Combine all ingredients in large saucepan.
Warm thoroughly, but do not boil.
Serve hot, in mugs, garnished with pear wedge.

Per serving: 227 Calories; 0g Fat (0% calories from fat); 0g Protein; 38g Carbohydrate; 0mg Cholesterol; 18mg Sodium

NOTES

_____

_____

_____

_____

_____

_____

_____

_____

Keuka Lake Wine Cooler

From McGregor Vineyard, Finger Lakes, New York

Serves 6

1 bottle Riesling wine
10 ounces bitter lemon soda
2 tablespoons orange liqueur
1 large peach, sliced
1 large nectarine, sliced
1 large orange, sliced
1 cup seedless grapes, green

A refreshing way to serve
McGregor Riesling.

Cut up fruit and marinate in wine and liqueur, chill. Add bitter lemon and ice just before serving.

Per serving: 60 Calories; 0g Fat (3% calories from fat); 1g Protein; 11g Carbohydrate; 0mg Cholesterol; 3mg Sodium

NOTES

_____

_____

_____

_____

_____

_____

_____

_____

Light and Fresh Sangria

From St. Julian Wine Co., Michigan

Serves 12

1 pint strawberries, unhulled
7 cups red wine semi-dry
1/2 lemon, thinly sliced
1/2 lime, thinly sliced
1 orange, thinly sliced
1 stick cinnamon
1 bottle sparkling white grape juice
fresh mint leaves for garnish

For your summer pleasure,
a refreshing mixture of
St. Julian Village Red and
Sparkling White Grape Juice.

Place one washed unhulled strawberry (hull up) in each compartment of two ice cube trays.

Pour in enough red wine to cover strawberries. Freeze.

Mix remaining ingredients in large glass pitcher or punch bowl.

In each individual glass add 2 frozen strawberries and pour sangria mixture over this.

Place remaining strawberries in sangria.

Garnish each glass with mint sprig.

Per serving: 113 Calories; 0g Fat (4% calories from fat); 1g Protein; 6g Carbohydrate; 0mg Cholesterol; 7mg Sodium

NOTES

_____

_____

_____

_____

_____

_____

Natural Fruit Champagne Cocktails

From Peterson and Sons Winery, Michigan

Serves 1

1 ounce fruit wine
3 ounces champagne from
the Great Lakes

These kir-type combinations hit the spot with the Naturally Old Fashioned fruit wines of Peterson and Sons.

Mix Raspberry, Cranberry, Cherry or Blueberry wine with a Great Lakes sparkling champagne.

Per serving: 72 Calories; 0g Fat (0% calories from fat); 0g Protein; 3g Carbohydrate; 0mg Cholesterol; 0mg Sodium

NOTES

_____

_____

_____

_____

_____

_____

_____

Strawberry or Peach Refresher

From Warner Vineyards, Michigan

Serves 8

1 bottle semi-dry white wine
1 bottle champagne brut
1 pint fresh strawberries or peaches,
  cut in tiny pieces
2 tablespoons sugar

A delightful Great Lakes summer treat when made with Warner Classic White and Brut Champagne.

Lightly sprinkle fruit with sugar and allow to stand for one hour.
Mix wine and champagne in a punch bowl. Add fruit and stir.
Serve in a large wine glass making sure to include a generous amount of fruit in each glass.

Per serving: 15 Calories; 0g Fat (0% calories from fat); 0g Protein; 3g Carbohydrate; 0mg Cholesterol; 0mg Sodium

NOTES

_____

_____

_____

_____

_____

_____

_____

_____

Summer Sangria

From Lemon Creek Winery, Michigan

Serves 10

1 bottle rosé wine, Lemon
   Creek Baco
1 liter soda water lemon-lime flavor
1 cup brandy
1 cup Triple Sec
 fresh fruit garnish

A refreshing beverage for guests.
Chill and enjoy!

    Cut your choice of fresh fruit into bite-size chunks. Fruit suggestions: Orange, apple, sweet cherries, grapes, cantelope, peaches, etc.

    Place your favorite combination of fruit chunks (about 1-2 cups) into a large pitcher along with the other ingredients.

Per serving: 67 Calories; 0g Fat (0% calories from fat); 0g Protein; 1g Carbohydrate; 0mg Cholesterol; 1mg Sodium

NOTES

_____

_____

_____

_____

_____

_____

_____

_____

Desserts

Cherry Brownies

From Lakeshore Winery, Finger Lakes, New York

Serves 16

4 ounces unsweetened baking chocolate
3/4 cup butter or margarine
1 3/4 cups sugar
1/4 cup cherry-flavored Jell-O mix
  (1/2 package)
3 large eggs
1 teaspoon vanilla extract
2 teaspoons dry red wine
1 cup all-purpose flour

The cherry flavor in these
brownies makes them
especially good with
Lakeshore Pinot Noir.

Preheat oven to 350 degrees F. and spray a 13-by-9 inch baking pan with non-stick spray.

Break chocolate into pieces along with butter in a microwave-safe bowl large enough to hold all ingredients. Microwave on high for about 2 minutes, until chocolate is melted. Stir until smooth. Measure Jell-O into a 2-cup measuring cup and fill to the 2-cup mark with sugar. Add the sugar and Jell-O to the chocolate mixture; stir until well-blended. Add eggs, vanilla and wine, stir again. Stir in the flour. Spread evenly in the prepared pan.

Bake for 30 to 35 minutes or until a wooden pick inserted in the center comes out clean. Cool and cut into squares.

Per serving: 635 Calories; 36g Fat (48% calories from fat); 7g Protein; 80g Carbohydrate; 152mg Cholesterol; 262mg Sodium

NOTES

_____

_____

_____

_____

_____

Cherry Delight

From Warner Vineyards, Michigan

Serves 4

1 envelope unflavored gelatin
   (1/4 ounce)
3 tablespoons sugar
3/4 cup water
1 cup cherry wine
2 cups whipped topping
1/2 cup milk

A little glass of Warner's Light Blush or Waterworks Station Cherry wine would go nicely with this light dessert.

Mix sugar with unflavored gelatin. Dissolve in 3/4 cup of boiling water. Remove from heat, stir in cherry wine. Let set until consistency of egg whites.

When gelatin mixture is ready, fold gently into whipped topping. (Add a little red food color to deepen the color, if you wish).

Spoon into parfait glasses with fresh cherries or into a graham cracker or baked pie shell. Finish off with more whipped topping and fresh fruit for an attractive presentation.

Per serving: 212 Calories; 6g Fat (25% calories from fat); 4g Protein; 37g Carbohydrate; 8mg Cholesterol; 97mg Sodium

NOTES

_____

_____

_____

_____

_____

_____

_____

Chocolate Raspberry Surprise

From McGregor Vineyard, Finger Lakes, New York

Serves 16

1 cup butter room temp.
1 1/4 cups sugar
1/2 cup packed brown sugar
4 large eggs
1/2 cup unsweetened cocoa powder
3 tablespoons raspberry liqueur
1 teaspoon vanilla
1/4 teaspoon salt
1 1/4 cups all-purpose flour
1 pint fresh raspberries
4 ounces semisweet chocolate
2 teaspoons hot water
powdered sugar

Raspberries and chocolate go great with a glass of McGregor Pinot Noir.

For brownies: preheat oven to 325 degrees F. Grease 9x13 inch pan. Beat butter, sugar and brown sugar in large bowl until fluffy. Add eggs one at at time, beating well after each addition. Stir in cocoa, 1 T. liqueur, vanilla and salt. Gently mix in flour. Pour batter into prepared pan. Sprinkle raspberries evenly over batter. Bake until tester inserted in center of brownies comes out clean, about 30 minutes. Cool completely in pan on rack.

For glaze: combine chocolate, 2 T. liqueur and water in top of double boiler. Set over barely simmering water and stir until smooth. Cool slightly.
Cut brownies. Sift powdered sugar lightly over them. Dip fork into glaze and drizzle decoratively over brownies. Let stand until glaze sets, about 30 minutes. Transfer brownies to plate and serve. May be prepared up to eight hours ahead. Cover and store at room temperature.

Per serving: 294 Calories; 15g Fat (45% calories from fat); 3g Protein; 38g Carbohydrate; 76mg Cholesterol; 167mg Sodium

NOTES

Double Chocolate Cheesecake with Raspberry Glaze

From St. Julian Wine Company, Michigan

Serves 12

9 ounces chocolate wafer cookies,
    finely crushed
1/2 cup butter or margarine, melted
3 tablespoons sugar
32 ounces cream cheese, softened
1 cup sugar
8 ounces sour cream
2 eggs
1 1/2 teaspoons vanilla or 3 T. cream sherry
2 tablespoons unsweetened cocoa powder
2 cups semisweet chocolate chips, melted
1/2 cup seedless red raspberry preserves
1/4 cup cream sherry

The critically acclaimed St. Julian Solera Cream Sherry is a key ingredient. And, St. Julian's Blanc de Blanc Champagne or Catherman's Port make excellent companions.

For crust: in a bowl, combine wafer crumbs, butter or margarine and sugar. Blend well. Press onto the bottom and 2 inches up the sides of a 9-inch springform pan. Set aside.

For filling: in a large mixing bowl, beat the cream cheese and 1 cup sugar with electric mixer until smooth. Add sour cream, eggs, vanilla or sherry and cocoa powder. Beat well. Beat in cooled chocolate. Pour into prepared crust, smoothing top of filling.

Place cheesecake in a springform pan. Bake in a 350 degrees F. oven for about 1 hour or until center appears nearly set when shaken. Remove from oven. Cool for 15 minutes. Loosen crust from sides of pan. Cool for 30 minutes more, remove sides of pan. Cool completely.

For glaze: in a small saucepan, stir together preserves and sherry over medium heat for 3 minutes. Remove from heat and cool. Carefully spread half of the glaze over cheesecake. Cover and chill at least 4 hours before serving.

Cut cheesecake into thin slices and drizzle with remaining glaze. Cover carefully and store in the refrigerator for up to 3 days.

Per serving: 688 Calories; 50g Fat (63% calories from fat); 10g Protein; 57g Carbohydrate; 142mg Cholesterol; 446mg Sodium

Easy and Elegant Trifle

From Arbor Hill Grapery, Finger Lakes, New York

Serves 6

10 ounces frozen strawberries or
   raspberries
3 ounces Jello mix (match fruit flavor)
3 ounces vanilla pudding mix, instant
1/2 cup Brahm's Sherry Wine Sauce
6 tablespoons whipped cream
angel food cake

Arbor Hill's Brahm's Sherry Wine Sauce is available, along with other wine products, directly from the Grapery (see the winery listing).

Dissolve Jello in boiling water. Add frozen berries and stir occasionally until thawed. Chill until slightly set. Make instant pudding. Arrange bite-size pieces of angel food cake in a clear trifle bowl and top with Sherry Wine Sauce.

Cover with a thin layer of Jello mixture, topped with a thin layer of pudding. Continue alternating layers until both Jello and pudding are used up. Top with whipped cream.

Chill for at least 3 hours. When ready to serve, spoon trifle into clear wine glasses or dessert dishes and top with a drizzle of Wine Sauce.

Per serving: 115 Calories; 3g Fat (21% calories from fat); 0g Protein; 23g Carbohydrate; 10mg Cholesterol; 110mg Sodium

NOTES

_____

_____

_____

_____

_____

_____

Fruit Whoopee!

From Joe Borrello

Serves 8

1/2 watermelon
1/2 pint fresh raspberries
1/2 pint fresh blueberries
1/2 pint fresh peaches, cubed
1/2 pint fresh strawberries
1/2 pint fresh cherries
1/2 cantaloupe, cubed
3/4 liter Riesling wine,
   semi-dry & chilled

This refreshing wine and fruit combination utilizes fresh fruit of the season and the fragrant, semi-dry wines of the Great Lakes.

Hollow out the half watermelon by making watermelon balls (avoiding the seeds as much as possible) and placing the balls in a bowl. Peel and cube the half cantalope after cleaning out the seeds.

Wash, de-stem and pit all other fruit and mix with the watermelon and cantalope. (It is much better to use fresh fruit as opposed to frozen or canned).

Return the fruit mixture to the hollowed-out watermelon shell and pour in the wine. Cover with plastic wrap and let marinade in the refrigerator for an hour or so. Serve chilled in your largest wine glasses for an elegant dessert or afternoon treat.

Use the watermelon shell and fruit for a table centerpiece...and second helpings.

Per serving: 179 Calories; 1g Fat (9% calories from fat); 2g Protein; 27g Carbohydrate; 0mg Cholesterol; 12mg Sodium

NOTES

_____

_____

_____

_____

Iced Champagne Sabayon

From Chef Izabela Kalabis, Inniskillin Winery, Ontario

Serves 2

1 cup vanilla ice cream
2 egg yolks
4 tablespoons sugar
2/3 cup champagne
1/2 cup whipping cream
fresh berries and mint for decoration

Inniskillin's L'Allemand Canadian Champagne is a natural partner for this delicate dessert.

A few hours before serving, combine egg yolks and sugar in a small saucepan. Place over low heat and whisk vigorously, slowly pouring in champagne.

Continue whisking until cream is frothy and thickens. Take off heat and let cool in refrigerator.

One half hour before serving, whip 1/2 cup cream until soft peaks form. Gently fold cream into chilled sabayon mixture. To serve, scoop ice cream into individual dishes, top with sabayon and decorate with fresh berries and mint.

Per serving: 561 Calories; 34g Fat (60% calories from fat); 6g Protein; 45g Carbohydrate; 323mg Cholesterol; 83mg Sodium

NOTES

_____

_____

_____

_____

_____

_____

_____

Iced Pear Souffle

From Chef Izabela Kalabis, Inniskillin Winery, Ontario

Serves 6

2 cups water
3/4 cup sugar
6 tablespoons fresh lemon juice
    (2 lemons)
1 vanilla bean split lengthwise
6 medium pears
1/3 cup water
2 teaspoons pear brandy
3/4 cup sugar
3 egg whites
1 cup whipping cream

> Only Inniskillin Icewine, Ontario's award-winning Icewine, should accompany this delectable dessert.

Prepare poaching syrup with water, sugar, lemon and vanilla bean. Peel and halve the pears, immerse in syrup and poach about 15 minutes. Let cool in syrup. Drain and puree the pears in a food processor, then pass through sieve, to make 2 1/4 cups of pear puree.

Add pear brandy and set aside. Bring to boil water and sugar in a heavy saucepan, cooking until mixture reaches soft ball stage. In a mixer beat egg whites until foaming, turn mixer to highest speed and slowly pour in hot syrup. Beat until cool and firm. Fold in pear puree. Whip cream until soft peaks form and set aside 1/4 cup for decoration. Fold remaining whipped cream into pear mixture. Pour pear mixture into dishes and put in freezer for 2 hours or until firm. Decorate with rosettes of whipped cream and crushed silver leaf.

Per serving: 437 Calories; 15g Fat (30% calories from fat); 3g Protein; 76g Carbohydrate; 54mg Cholesterol; 46mg Sodium

NOTES

_____

_____

_____

Icewine Truffles

From London Winery, Ontario

Serves 36

1/3 cup whipping cream
1/2 pound semisweet chocolate,
    finely chopped
1/3 cup sweet dessert wine, "Icewine"
2 tablespoons butter softened
1/4 cup cocoa powder
1 teaspoon powdered sugar

A delectable treat and
perfect companion with
London Winery's Icewine
for an exquisite finish to a
wonderful meal.

Bring cream to boil and add to chocolate in a bowl. Blend, then stir in Icewine.

Beat in butter when cool. Set aside until firm enough to handle, then drop mixture by small spoonfuls into a shallow dish of cocoa powder sweetened to taste with powdered sugar.

Roll each truffle in cocoa, rounding it between the palms of your hands. Dust hands with cocoa as necessary to keep truffles from sticking. If truffles are too hard to shape, wait until they soften. If they are too soft, chill until firm. Truffles look more authentic if they are a little irregular in shape.

Shake truffles gently in a dry strainer, if necessary, to remove excess cocoa.

Store in an airtight container in the refrigerator for up to 10 days or in freezer for up to 3 months. Remove from refrigerator 30 minutes before serving to soften slightly.

Serve in a candy dish or place each truffle in a fluted paper cup. Makes 3 dozen small truffles.

Per serving: 48 Calories; 3g Fat (60% calories from fat); 0g Protein; 5g Carbohydrate; 5mg Cholesterol; 8mg Sodium

NOTES

_____

_____

_____

_____

Late Harvest Gewurztraminer Cake

From McGregor Vineyard, Finger Lakes, New York

Serves 16

18 ounces yellow cake mix,
   Duncan Hines
1 package vanilla pudding, instant
1/2 cup water
1 cup sweet white wine,
   Gewurztraminer
1/2 cup vegetable oil
4 eggs
1/2 cup pecans, chopped
1/4 pound butter
1 cup sugar
1/4 cup water

A unique dessert treat with McGregor Late Harvest Gewurztraminer or Vignoles.

Line bottom of greased 10" tube pan with chopped pecans. Blend boxed cake mix, pudding, water, 1/2 cup of wine, oil and eggs with mixer and pour into pecan-lined tube pan. Bake at 325 degrees F. for 50-60 minutes.

Mix and boil for 3 minutes: butter, sugar and 1/4 cup of water. Remove from heat and then add remaining 1/2 cup of wine. Pour this mixture over hot cake and leave in pan 30 minutes before turning out.

Per serving: 334 Calories; 19g Fat (50% calories from fat); 3g Protein; 39g Carbohydrate; 62mg Cholesterol; 292mg Sodium

NOTES

_____

_____

_____

_____

Mr. G's Catawabapple

From Paramount Distillers, Ohio

Serves 1

1 small apple,
  core & cut into $1/8$'s
8 ounces Catawba wine,
  chilled

Here, unquestionably, is the world's fastest and easiest dessert with a Catawba wine from Meier's, Mantey, Lonz or Mon Ami.

Gather the sectioned apples together to form the original whole apple (without the core) and place it carefully in a large wine glass allowing the sections to spread, petal-like, against the edges. Pour on the well-iced Pink or White Catawba wine.

Per serving: 75 Calories; 0g Fat (5% calories from fat); 0g Protein; 19g Carbohydrate; 0mg Cholesterol; 0mg Sodium

NOTES

No-Fat Peach Dessert

From Fenn Valley Vineyards, Michigan

Serves 6

10 medium fresh peaches, ripe
1 cup apple juice
1 cup peach wine
1 teaspoon cinnamon
1 teaspoon white wine vinegar
4 teaspoons cornstarch
1/4 cup water

A "peach" of a dessert when served with Fenn Valley Vineyard Nectar or Late Harvest Vignoles.

Pit and slice all but 1 peach. Put the slices into 6 individual serving bowls and place in the freezer. If possible, freeze the peach slices for at least 30 minutes before adding the hot sauce.

Mix cornstarch in 1/4 cup of water.

Combine the apple juice, peach wine and cinnamon in a saute or sauce pan and bring to a boil. While the wine and juice are being reduced, skin and puree the last peach. Add the pureed peach to the pan and continue to boil gently.

When the volume is reduced to about half of the starting volume, add the vinegar. Slowly add the cornstarch mixture, stirring constantly, until the sauce is thickened.

Pour the sauce over the chilled peaches and serve immediately.

Per serving: 75 Calories; 0g Fat (2% calories from fat); 1g Protein; 19g Carbohydrate; 0mg Cholesterol; 2mg Sodium

NOTES

_____

_____

_____

_____

_____

Peach and Mascarpone Mousse in Phyllo

From Chef Erik Peacock, Henry of Pelham Winery, Ontario

Serves 4

1/2 cup unsalted butter, melted
1/2 cup sugar
3 whole peaches, peeled
1/4 cup water
1/2 lemon, freshly squeezed
4 eggs
1 cup whipping cream
1/4 cup mascarpone cheese
3/4 cup almonds, whole
3 sheets phyllo pastry
2 poached peaches, optional

The raves from your dinner guests make this dessert worth the effort; add a glass of Henry of Pelham Late Harvest Seyval or Icewine.

Melt 1/4 cup of butter in medium size saucepan. Dissolve sugar and add skinless flesh of peaches over low heat. Add water and lemon juice and cook for approximately 8-10 minutes or until flesh is quite soft. Remove from heat and crack eggs into the food processor. Blend for a second or two. Add the hot peaches and syrup mixture to eggs in processor and blend until smooth and combined. In the same saucepan, add blended peaches and eggs and cook over medium heat until it thickens to a custard, or about 15 minutes. This mixture should coat the back of a wooden spoon. Empty contents of saucepan into stainless steel bowl and prepare an ice water bath in a second bowl. Place the peach custard bowl in the ice water bath and cool completely. While this is chilling, take 3 tablespoons of the whipping cream and whisk it into the cream cheese to soften it. Whip the rest of the cream and keep chilled. When the custard is chilled, fold in the mascarpone until incorporated. When this is done, fold the whipped cream in, cover and chill for at least 2 hours or overnight.

PHYLLO PASTRY CUPS

Preheat oven to 350 degrees F. and toast almonds on cookie sheet. In a food processor, grind almonds to a coarse meal. Take 4 sheets of phyllo and divide them evenly by 4, producing 16 rectangles. Brush on some melted butter and cover with a damp towel to prevent the pastry from drying out.

Each pastry cup will use 4 rectangles and in between each layer will be a sprinkle of ground almond.

On your work suface lay out 4 single rectangles of phyllo and brush each with butter. Sprinkle with nuts and repeat 2 more times. Place the layered phyllo in a muffin tin or equivalent and bake at 350 degrees F. Set a timer for 6 minutes. When the cups are done they will be golden brown. These may be made a day ahead and stored uncovered on the counter.

To assemble this dessert, have slices of poached peach to sit the cups on. Fill the cups with the peach and mascarpone mousse and serve by itself or with another fruit puree to provide some color on the plate.

Per serving: 742 Calories; 60g Fat (71% calories from fat); 11g Protein; 44g Carbohydrate; 338mg Cholesterol; 155mg Sodium

NOTES

_____

_____

_____

_____

_____

_____

_____

_____

Poached Apples

From Chef Erik Peacock, Henry of Pelham Winery, Ontario

Serves 4

3 Granny Smith apples	The simplicity of Great Lakes fruit and
1 cup dry white wine	a bottle of Henry of Pelham Riesling on a
2 1/2 cups water	fall picnic is what life is all about.
1 stick cinnamon	

Peel apples, cut in quarters and core.

Bring wine and water to a boil with cinnamon stick in the liquid. Add the apple quarters and simmer for approximately 15 minutes or until tender.

Remove from pot when finished and set aside to cool - discard poaching liquid.

Serve with ice cream, a favorite custard cream or on top of DUCK LIVER PATE sitting on folded GREEN ONION CREPES and covered with a DUCK BREAST IN A BLACK CURRANT GLAZE (see recipe) for an elegant luncheon entree.

Per serving: 91 Calories; 0g Fat (2% calories from fat); 0g Protein; 14g Carbo-hydrate; 0mg Cholesterol; 10mg Sodium

NOTES

_____

_____

_____

_____

_____

_____

_____

Raspberry Lovers' Super Dessert

From Peterson and Sons Winery, Michigan

Serves 1

1/4 cup fresh raspberries
1/4 cup raspberry wine
3/4 cup vanilla ice cream

It may be fattening, but it sure is good with Peterson and Sons Raspberry wine.

    Place fresh raspberries in a glass container and cover with raspberry wine. Seal container and let sit 24 hours in refrigerator.

    Pour mix over premium vanilla ice cream which has been placed in a tulip-style wine glass or blend the ice cream and mix in a blender for a Super Shake!

Per serving: 213 Calories; 11g Fat (45% calories from fat); 4g Protein; 27g Carbohydrate; 44mg Cholesterol; 79mg Sodium

NOTES

_____

_____

_____

_____

_____

_____

_____

_____

Ravat Blanc Mousse

From Wagner Vineyards/Ginny Lee Cafe, Finger Lakes, New York

Serves 6

1 envelope gelatin, unflavored
3/4 cup cold water
1/4 cup sugar
3/4 cup pineapple juice
2 tablespoons sweet white wine
2 cups whipped topping

Serve this light dessert in a champagne flute or wine glass topped with whipped cream, a pineapple chunk and a mint leaf. Wagner Vineyards Ravat Blanc Icewine wine is the perfect match for this treat.

Sprinkle gelatin (1 envelope = 1/4 ounce) over 3/4 cup cold water in small saucepan; let stand 1 minute. Cook over low heat, stirring until gelatin dissolves, about 2 minutes. Add 1/4 cup sugar and pineapple juice to gelatin mixture. Cook until sugar dissolves, 2-3 minutes. Transfer to a large bowl. Add wine, stirring well. Cover and chill for 25 minutes or until consistency of unbeaten egg whites. Beat gelatin mixture at high speed until light and fluffy. Cover and chill for 20 minutes. Gently fold in whipped topping. Chill at least 2 hours.

Per serving: 107 Calories; 3g Fat (28% calories from fat); 2g Protein; 18g Carbohydrate; 3mg Cholesterol; 22mg Sodium

NOTES

_____

_____

_____

_____

_____

_____

Red Wine Raspberry Sorbet

From St. Julian Wine Company, Michigan

Serves 6

3 cups raspberries, fresh or
  frozen
1 1/4 cups dry red wine
1 1/2 tablespoons fresh lemon juice
3/4 cup sugar
1/2 cup whipping cream

This recipe won the dessert division
in a local newspaper recipe contest
with St. Julian Village Red wine as
the secret ingredient.

Place all ingredients in a food processor fitted with a steel blade and process until smooth. Freeze in an ice cream maker. Let set in refrigerator 15-20 minutes before serving.

Per serving: 230 Calories; 8g Fat (33% calories from fat); 1g Protein; 34g Carbohydrate; 27mg Cholesterol; 10mg Sodium

NOTES

_____

_____

_____

_____

_____

_____

_____

_____

Riesling Cake

From Reif Estate Winery, Ontario

Serves 16

CAKE
1 cup butter or margarine, unsalted
1 1/4 cups sugar
2 cups all-purpose flour
4 eggs
1 teaspoon vanilla
1 tablespoon cinnamon
1/2 cup Riesling wine, late harvest
1 teaspoon baking powder
2 tablespoons bread crumbs

Enjoy this "grapelicious" cake together with Reif Riesling Late Harvest.

FILLING
1 1/2 packages vanilla pudding mix, regular size
2 cups Riesling wine, late harvest
1/2 teaspoon vanilla extract
5 tablespoons sugar
1 1/2 teaspoons cinnamon
1 teaspoon gelatin powder
2 cups whipping cream or whipped topping
3/4 cup powdered sugar, sifted

PREPARE CAKE
   Mix and prepare batter. Put in a spring-form pan basted with margarine or butter and sprinkled with bread crumbs. Bake in oven at 325 degrees F. for approximately 45-50 minutes. Remove from oven and let cool, then slice into 3 layers.

PREPARE FILLING
   Mix dry pudding, wine, vanilla, sugar and cinnamon and bring to a slow boil. Soften gelatin powder in cold water then dissolve it in the hot filling mixture. Let cool.
   Prepare whipping cream to a point of being stiff and stir gently into the cool filling mixture. Stuff layers with filling.
   Mix powered sugar and enough of the wine to create a glaze for the cake. Garnish with grapes.

Per serving: 441 Calories; 24g Fat (50% calories from fat); 4g Protein; 49g Carbohydrate; 117mg Cholesterol; 245mg Sodium

Tiramisu

From Chef Tom Johnson, Meier's Winery, Ohio

Serves 12

24 ladyfinger cookies, split
1 1/2 cups cream sherry
10 large egg yolks
1 pinch salt
1/2 cup granulated sugar
1 pound mascarpone cheese
2 cups whipping cream
3 tablespoons unsweetened cocoa
   powder for garnish

The key ingredient to this lovely dessert is the Meier's #44 Cream Sherry. Do not substitute with a dry, pale sherry.

Line a 13x9x2-inch glass baking dish with half of the split ladyfingers. Brush them with 1/2 cup of the cream sherry. Set aside to prepare the custard.

In a heavy bottomed, acid-resistant saucepan, cook the egg yolks, blended with 1/4 cup of the cream sherry, over medium heat until they are barely thickened and lustrous, but not solidified. Using a rubber spatula, turn these yolks into the bowl of a stand mixer. Add the pinch of salt and the granulated sugar and whisk at low speed to blend, gradually increasing to high speed. Beat at high speed until the mixture is thick and pale lemon colored...about 5 minutes. Then, lower the speed and blend in the mascarpone cheese and another 1/4 cup of cream sherry. Increase speed and whip until well-blended and smooth. Reserve.

In another mixing bowl, well-chilled, with a clean, well-chilled whisk attachment, whip the cream at medium speed until soft peaks are formed. Fold the whipped cream into the mascarpone-egg mixture. Carefully blend, taking care not to deflate the air from this mixture.

Using a rubber spatula, evenly smooth half of the custard mixture on top of the ladyfingers in the glass dish. Distribute the remaining ladyfingers on top of the first layer of custard. Brush them with the remaining 1/2 cup of cream sherry. Smooth the remaining custard evenly on top of the second layer of lady fingers. Wrap tightly and chill for at least 6 hours.

To serve, unwrap and sieve cocoa powder over the top of the Tiramisu.

Per serving: 473 Calories; 39g Fat (73% calories from fat); 8g Protein; 25g Carbohydrate; 364mg Cholesterol; 87mg Sodium

Tropical Fruit Kebabs with Caramel Sauce

From Fenn Valley Vineyards, Michigan

Serves 6

1 large mango, peeled and cubed
1/2 papaya, ripe, seed, peel & cube
1 medium pineapple, skin, core & cube
1 large orange, 1/2" slices-quarters
1/4 cup lime juice
2 tablespoons dark rum
2 teaspoons vanilla extract
1 cup white wine semi-sweet
1/4 cup brown sugar firmly packed
6 whole cloves
1 stick cinnamon

Different and delicious, especially with a luscious glass of Fenn Valley Vineyard Nectar.

Place about 1 cup of the smaller or odd-shaped mango and papaya chunks with lime juice, rum and vanilla in the food processor. Process until smooth; set aside.

Combine wine, brown sugar, cloves and cinnamon in medium sauce pan and cook over medium heat for 12-15 minutes. Increase heat to medium-high and cook for 10 more minutes (do not stir). Remove from heat and let stand for 1 minute. Discard cloves and cinnamon stick. Slowly stir in mango/papaya mixture. Set aside.

Thread remaining mango & papaya cubes, pineapple and orange wedges on 6 skewers, alternating each fruit. Grill or broil for 8 minutes until lightly browned, basting occasionally with caramel sauce. Serve with remaining sauce.

Per serving: 177 Calories; 2g Fat (11% calories from fat); 1g Protein; 35g Carbohydrate; 0mg Cholesterol; 23mg Sodium

NOTES

_____

_____

Zabaglione

From Old Firehouse Winery, Ohio

Serves 2

4 egg yolks
2 tablespoons powdered sugar
3 tablespoons red wine, semi-dry

A simple recipe using Old Firehouse Red for this tasty Italian dessert.

In the bottom of a double-boiler, bring water to hot, but do not let it boil.

Combine the yolks and sugar in the top of the double boiler. Beat constantly using a high-quality French whip or electric beater.

While beating, slowly mix in the wine. Keep beating until mixture begins to hold its shape, but is still smooth. Pile immediately into heated thick cups. Be careful not to scrape sides of boiler if the mixture is overheated, the crust on the bowl will ruin the texture. If the mixture separated, it has been either over-heated or over-whipped.

Serve either warm or cooled with simple wafers.

Per serving: 164 Calories; 10g Fat (62% calories from fat); 6g Protein; 8g Carbohydrate; 425mg Cholesterol; 15mg Sodium

NOTES

_____

_____

_____

_____

_____

_____

_____

Dips & Sauces

Bourdelaise Sauce

From Old Firehouse Winery, Ohio

Serves 8

1 teaspoon ground pepper
1 small bay leaf
1/4 medium onion
1 pinch thyme
1 cup red wine, semi-dry
1 cup broth (beef, pork or chicken)
1/2 teaspoon salt
1 teaspoon cornstarch
1 tablespoon parsley
2 tablespoons butter
1 pinch marjoram
1 teaspoon lemon juice

A favorite winery variation is to add mushrooms to the simmering wine sauce, but there is no substitute for Firehouse Red wine.

Place onion quarter in a saucepan with wine, herbs, spices, salt and pepper. Simmer on low until the quantity is reduced by half, which takes about 20 minutes.

Add the cup of broth, but hold back about 2 tablespoons for later use. Keep burner on low until the liquid is again reduced by half. Remove onion. Add the lemon juice, butter and parsley to the sauce.

Take the remaining 2 tablespoons of cold broth and add cornstarch. Stir. Combine the cold broth/cornstarch mix with the warm sauce and heat until slightly thickened.

Serve over the meat that corresponds with the broth.

Per serving: 51 Calories; 3g Fat (77% calories from fat); 0g Protein; 2g Carbohydrate; 8mg Cholesterol; 183mg Sodium

NOTES

_____

_____

_____

Fondue for Two

**From Castel Crisch Winery & Restaurant,
Finger Lakes, New York**

Serves 2

3/4 cup Chardonnay
1 teaspoon lemon juice
1/4 pound Emmenthaler cheese, shredded or diced
1/4 pound gruyere cheese, shredded or diced
white pepper to taste
nutmeg to taste
1 loaf French bread, 1 inch cubes

Castel Grisch
Chardonnay makes
the perfect match
with Swiss fondue.

Toast cubed bread very lightly on a flat baking sheet in oven, keep warm.

While toasting bread, heat wine over medium flame in proper pot until wine is hot, but not boiling. Add lemon juice. Add cheese in small batches, stirring constantly.

Mix until cheese and wine blend into a creamy sauce. Add pepper and nutmeg.

Bring mixture to a boil and remove pot to a lighted table burner.

Dip toasted French bread into cheese and enjoy.

*Per serving: 543 Calories; 34g Fat (64% calories from fat); 34g Protein; 10g
Carbohydrate; 114mg Cholesterol; 419mg Sodium*

NOTES

_____

_____

_____

_____

_____

_____

Fruit Dip

From Arbor Hill Grapery, Finger Lakes, New York

Serves 4

1/2 cup sour cream or mayonnaise
1/4 cup Brahm's Sherry Wine Sauce,
   * see note
1 1/2 teaspoons lemon juice

This simple Arbor Hill dip may also be used as a sauce on pound cake for dessert.

    In a small bowl whisk together all ingredients. Use as a dip for skewered fresh fruits.

    *A catalog of Arbor Hill jellies, sauces, vinegars and preserves is available directly from the Grapery (see the winery listing).

Per serving: 62 Calories; 6g Fat (85% calories from fat); 1g Protein; 1g Carbohydrate; 13mg Cholesterol; 15mg Sodium

NOTES

_____

_____

_____

_____

_____

_____

_____

_____

Great Lakes Vineyard Barbecue Sauce

From Chef Tom Johnson, Lonz Winery, Ohio

Serves 20

24 ounces red wine, sweet Concord
1/4 cup soy sauce
1/4 cup honey
1/4 cup ketchup
1/4 cup Dijon mustard
1 clove garlic, finely minced
1 tablespoon ginger, finely minced
1/2 teaspoon Tabasco sauce
1/4 cup cornstarch
1/4 cup port wine

A finger-lickin' good barbecue sauce. For a unique twist, try a bottle of Lonz Blackberry wine in place of Lonz Concord.

Combine all of the ingredients, except the cornstarch and port wine. Bring to a high simmer over medium-high heat. Simmer until reduced by 1/3.

Make a slurry of the cornstarch and the port wine. Slowly stir the slurry into the simmering sauce until it has reached desired thickness. Simmer an additional 5 minutes, then use to baste meat.

Per serving: 56 Calories; 0g Fat (4% calories from fat); 0g Protein; 7g Carbohydrate; 0mg Cholesterol; 241mg Sodium

NOTES

_____

_____

_____

_____

_____

_____

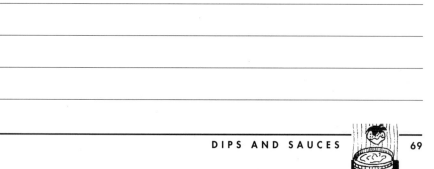

Green Fish Sauce

From Leelanau Cellars, Michigan

Serves 8

2 medium eggs
1 teaspoon Dijon mustard
1/4 teaspoon pepper
1 teaspoon salt
6 scallions with tops
1 clove garlic minced
1/4 teaspoon horseradish
3 tablespoons parsley, chopped
2 tablespoons fresh dill
1/2 cup spinach leaves (optional)
1/2 cup watercress (optional)
2 tablespoons lemon juice
1 1/2 cups vegetable oil

Serve with poached Lake Michigan trout and Leelanau Cellars Renaissance or Winter White.

Put eggs in blender or food processor. Add green items as desired or as season permits. Blend until smooth and pureed. Add garlic and lemon juice and blend for 10 seconds. Slowly, in a thin stream, pour in the oil, adding as much oil as will mix in. Add mustard, horseradish, salt and pepper, taste and adjust as desired.

Per serving: 391 Calories; 42g Fat (95% calories from fat); 2g Protein; 3g Carbohydrate; 45mg Cholesterol; 301mg Sodium

NOTES

_____

_____

_____

_____

_____

London Curry Dip

From London Winery, Ontario

Serves 12

1 1/2 cups mayonnaise-type salad dressing,
    Hellman's®
1 medium onion, grated
1/2 teaspoon pepper
3 tablespoons yogurt or sour cream
2 tablespoons sweet sherry
2 dashes Tabasco sauce
2 teaspoons curry powder
1/2 teaspoon dry mustard

Put this dip out at a party and watch how quickly it disappears. London Oxford Sherry is our wine of choice.

Blend all ingredients together, mix well. Serve with your favorite chips or crackers.

Per serving: 124 Calories; 10g Fat (72% calories from fat); 1g Protein; 8g Carbohydrate; 8mg Cholesterol; 257mg Sodium

NOTES

_____

_____

_____

_____

_____

_____

_____

Low-Fat Mustard Dill Sauce

From Fenn Valley Vineyards, Michigan

Serves 6

1 cup fresh dill, minced
3/8 cup dry white wine
3/8 cup nonfat sour cream
2 1/2 tablespoons Dijon mustard
1/8 teaspoon white pepper

This is a great topping for fish with Fenn Valley Lakeshore White on the table.

   Spray a non-stick pan lightly with olive oil. Saute the dill over med-high heat for 1-2 minutes until limp and fragrant.
   Add the wine and reduce to approximately 1 tablespoon of liquid. Remove from the heat.
   Add the sour cream, mustard and pepper. Stir. May be served immediately, but the dill flavor becomes more pronounced if the sauce is allowed to sit for 12 or more hours in the refrigerator before re-heating and serving.

Per serving: 51 Calories; 1g Fat (13% calories from fat); 2g Protein; 8g Carbohydrate; 2mg Cholesterol; 116mg Sodium

NOTES

_____

_____

_____

_____

_____

_____

_____

_____

Mustard Veggie Dip

From Lakeshore Winery, Finger Lakes, New York

Serves 10

16 ounces Miracle Whip® light
1/4 cup prepared mustard
1 cup sugar
1 tablespoon garlic powder
1 tablespoon Riesling wine

A hit at any party... both the dip and Lakeshore Johannisberg Riesling.

Mix all ingredients together. Let stand at least one hour and mix again. Chill and serve with sliced raw vegetables such as carrots, celery, broccoli, cauliflower, zucchini or cucumber. Store up to 4 weeks in the refrigerator.

Note: Do not be tempted to substitute real mayonnaise, as it does not contain enough water to dissolve the sugar.

Per serving: 228 Calories; 13g Fat (50% calories from fat); 1g Protein; 28g Carbohydrate; 10mg Cholesterol; 387mg Sodium

NOTES

_____

_____

_____

_____

_____

_____

_____

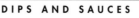

Not Enough Shrimp Dip

From Chalet Debonne Winery, Ohio

Serves 10

16 ounces cream cheese, softened
1/4 cup onion, chopped
1/4 cup celery, chopped
16 ounces salad shrimp,
   rinsed and drained
2 tablespoons Riesling wine

This dip is great with Pepperidge Farm Fish Crackers or Nabisco Waverly Crackers and Chalet Debonne Country Selections White or Lake Erie Johannisberg Riesling.

Set cream cheese out for a couple of hours before use.

Chop the celery and onion, rinse the shrimp and add all ingredients including the wine to large bowl and mix with wisk.

Fold into a serving dish and chill at least 6 hours before serving.

Per serving: 206 Calories; 16g Fat (72% calories from fat); 13g Protein; 1g Carbohydrate; 138mg Cholesterol; 253mg Sodium

NOTES

_____

_____

_____

_____

_____

_____

_____

Red Onion Tartar Sauce

From Chef Tom Johnson, Mon Ami Winery and Restaurant, Ohio

Serves 8

1 large red onion, quartered
3 eggs, hard-boiled, halved
1/2 cup India relish, drained
2 tablespoons capers, well-rinsed
1 1/2 cups mayonnaise, Hellman's®
1/4 teaspoon cayenne pepper
1 tablespoon tarragon vinegar

The perfect topping for Great Lakes fish along with a glass of Mon Ami American Chablis.

Place the quartered red onion in the work bowl of a food processor. Pulse on and off until the onion is finely minced. Add the halved hard-boiled eggs and pulse on and off three times to chop. Add the India relish and the capers, pulsing 5 times to blend. Add the mayonnaise, cayenne pepper and tarragon vinegar, pulsing on and off to blend.

Per serving: 328 Calories; 34g Fat (93% calories from fat); 3g Protein; 3g Carbohydrate; 92mg Cholesterol; 274mg Sodium

NOTES

_____

_____

_____

_____

_____

_____

_____

_____

Spinach-Artichoke Dip

From Buccia Vineyard, Ohio

Serves 8

16 ounces frozen spinach, thawed & chopped
8 ounces nonfat cream cheese
1 can artichokes, cut in small pieces
3 tablespoons dry white wine
1/4 cup Parmesan cheese, grated
1/2 teaspoon garlic salt

A party favorite when accompanied by a glass of Buccia Seyval wine.

Mix all ingredients in microwaveable bowl. Heat 2 minutes. Stir. Reheat if needed.

Serve with white baked tortilla chips.

Per serving: 66 Calories; 1g Fat (14% calories from fat); 8g Protein; 6g Carbohydrate; 6mg Cholesterol; 260mg Sodium

NOTES

_____

_____

_____

_____

_____

_____

_____

_____

Tomato & Curry Sauce/Marinade

From Fenn Valley Vineyards, Michigan

Serves 8

1 cup tomato sauce
1 cup white wine, semi-dry
1 tablespoon soy sauce
1 1/2 teaspoons white wine vinegar
3 cloves garlic, crushed
1/2 cup raisins
1 tablespoon curry powder
1 teaspoon ground turmeric
1/2 teaspoon ground allspice
1 teaspoon ground cinnamon
1 teaspoon ground marjoram

A spicy red sauce that adds life to rice and lean white meats. Serve with Fenn Valley Chancellor.

Mix all of the ingredients together in a glass bowl. Heat for 2 minutes in a microwave on high heat. Stir well and allow to cool.

If used as a marinade, add the meat (up to 8 chicken breasts or 10 pork tenderloin medallions) to the cooled mixture and let set 6-10 hours in refrigerator. Remove meat from marinade and grill.

For a sauce, reduce the mixture by gently boiling in a flat pan while stirring constantly. Serve over rice and/or cooked meat.

Per serving: 64 Calories; 0g Fat (5% calories from fat); 1g Protein; 11g Carbohydrate; 0mg Cholesterol; 292mg Sodium

NOTES

_____

_____

_____

_____

_____

_____

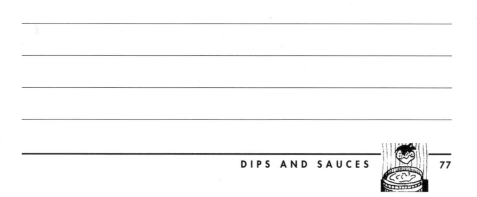

Wasabi Sauce

From Bowers Harbor Vineyards, Michigan

Serves 15

1 pint mayonnaise
1/4 pound spinach blanched
1/4 ounce Wasabi powder
1/4 cup horseradish, strained

Great on just about any seafood and served with a glass of Bowers Harbor Sparkling wine.

Steam spinach for 30 seconds in perforated pan.
Place all ingredients in food processor. Blend until smooth.
Cover, label and date.

Per serving: 213 Calories; 23g Fat (96% calories from fat); 1g Protein; 1g Carbohydrate; 17mg Cholesterol; 176mg Sodium

NOTES

_____

_____

_____

_____

_____

_____

_____

_____

Wild Mushroom Saute

From Fox Run Vineyards, Finger Lakes, New York

Serves 6

1 ounce dried wild mushrooms, mixed
1 1/2 cups water, warmed
4 tablespoons butter
4 tablespoons flour
8 ounces milk, hot
1/4 cup dry white wine
1 pound button mushrooms, fresh, sliced
1 tablespoon butter
1 tablespoon oil
1/4 cup onion, chopped
1 clove garlic, minced
salt and pepper to taste

Here's a sauce that creates a rich pasta entree or a tasty topping for beef or veal. Fox Run Blanc de Blanc will complement either.

Soak dried wild mushroom mix in 1 1/2 cups warmed water. Stir occasionally so any sand goes to the bottom of the water.

For cream sauce, mix butter with flour. Stir over heat until it smells like a freshly baked cookie, but not browned.

Add the hot milk and 6 ounces of water from the dried mushrooms. Stir and cook until it barely simmers, about 3-5 minutes. Add the wine, salt and pepper.

Saute the fresh mushrooms in 1 tablespoon each of butter and oil (peanut or canola) until slices brown and evaporate a lot of moisture from the mushrooms. Add the onion, garlic and softened dried mushrooms.

Saute onions until they start to brown. Add cream sauce and simmer 2-3 minutes.

Per serving: 173 Calories; 13g Fat (69% calories from fat); 3g Protein; 10g Carbohydrate; 31mg Cholesterol; 464mg Sodium

NOTES

_____

_____

Wine Sauce Barbecue for Beef

From Arbor Hill Grapery, Finger Lakes, New York

Serves 4

1/4 cup Brahm's Claret Wine Sauce
1/4 cup low sodium soy sauce
2 tablespoons garlic powder
1 teaspoon fresh ground pepper

A catalog of Arbor Hill wines, jellies, sauces, vinegars and preserves is available directly from the Grapery (see the winery listing).

Mix all ingredients and baste on cooking meat for the last two minutes before serving.

Per serving: 23 Calories; 0g Fat (2% calories from fat); 2g Protein; 5g Carbohydrate; 0mg Cholesterol; 485mg Sodium

NOTES

_____

_____

_____

_____

_____

_____

_____

Wine Sauce Barbecue for Poultry

From Arbor Hill Grapery, Finger Lakes, New York

Serves 4

1/4 cup Brahm's Sherry Wine Sauce
1/4 cup low sodium soy sauce
1/4 cup spicy mustard, dark
1 teaspoon garlic powder

A catalog of Arbor Hill sauces, jellies, vinegars and preserves is available directly from the Grapery (see the winery listing).

Mix all ingredients and baste on cooking meat for the last two minutes before serving.

Per serving: 24 Calories; 1g Fat (37% calories from fat); 2g Protein; 3g Carbohydrate; 0mg Cholesterol; 688mg Sodium

NOTES

_____

_____

_____

_____

_____

_____

_____

_____

Wine Sauce for Fish

From Lemon Creek Winery, Michigan

Serves 4

6 tablespoons low-fat mayonnaise
2 tablespoons lemon juice
6 tablespoons dry white wine, Vignoles
4 scallions sliced
2 sprigs parsley, chopped fine
 salt and pepper to taste

A low fat meal with rice pilaf, steamed vegetables and a glass of Lemon Creek Dry Vignoles.

   Combine lemon juice, mayonnaise and wine. Place fish in a large baking dish, lightly buttered. Pour sauce on top of fish. Top with scallions, parsley and seasonings.
   Cover and bake in a preheated oven at 350 degrees F. for 30 minutes.

Per serving: 181 Calories; 9g Fat (43% calories from fat); 7g Protein; 19g Carbohydrate; 0mg Cholesterol; 305mg Sodium

NOTES

_____

_____

_____

_____

_____

_____

_____

Fish &
Seafood

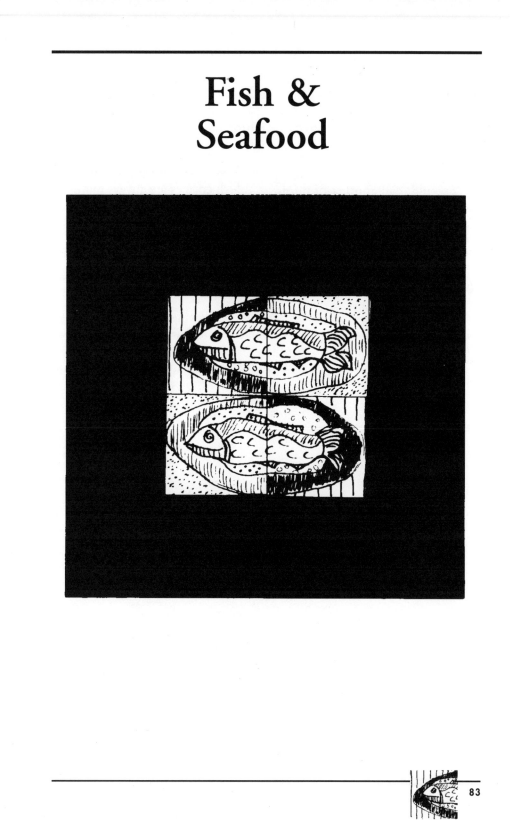

Baked Fish in Wine

From Fenn Valley Vineyards, Michigan

Serves 4

1 1/2 pounds cod or other firm fish
1 can cream of celery soup
2/3 can dry white wine, measure
  in soup can
2 tablespoons fresh parsley, chopped
salt and pepper, to taste
1/4 cup grated Parmesan cheese

Fish entrees are always more enjoyable with a glass of Fenn Valley Lakeshore White or Chardonel.

    Place fish in a glass baking dish. Pour soup and wine over the fish. Sprinkle with parsley and salt and pepper. Sprinkle generously with grated parmesan cheese.

    Bake covered for 30 minutes at 350 degrees F. Remove cover and bake an additional 10 minutes to brown.

Per serving: 189 Calories; 4g Fat (20% calories from fat); 33g Protein; 3g Carbohydrate; 81mg Cholesterol; 424mg Sodium

NOTES

_____

_____

_____

_____

_____

_____

_____

_____

Baked Stuffed Lake Trout

From L. Mawby Vineyards, Michigan

Serves 10

10 each lake trout fresh fillets

MARINADE:
1 tablespoon lemon juice
2 tablespoons dry white wine
 pinch tarragon
 pinch rosemary
3 tablespoons olive oil
3 cloves garlic, pressed

A delicious Great Lakes
dish with L. Mawby
Vignoles wine.

STUFFING:
1/2 pound butter
2 cups celery, finely chopped
2 cups onion, finely chopped
1 1/2 teaspoons sage
1 teaspoon herbal salt substitute
1/4 teaspoon black pepper
4 cups dried bread, cubed

Mix marinade ingredients and rub into skin of fish. Place fish in shallow baking dish. Pour remaining marinade over fish, cover and refrigerate for 24 hours. Turn fish after 12 hours.

Saute stuffing ingredients (minus bread) in butter until wilted. Pour over bread cubes, mix well. Place stuffing in fish. Return fish to dish with marinade and add additional wine to bring liquid level in dish to 1/4 inch.

Bake covered at 350 degrees F. for 1 1/4 hours or until desired doneness.

Per serving: 566 Calories; 32g Fat (51% calories from fat); 30g Protein; 39g Carbohydrate; 116mg Cholesterol; 1147mg Sodium

NOTES

Barbecue Fish - Keuka Lake Style

From McGregor Vineyard, Finger Lakes, New York

Serves 6

4 pounds freshwater fillets

SAUCE
1 cup dry white wine
3/4 cup lemon juice
1/8 pound butter
2 tablespoons Worcestershire sauce
1 teaspoon hot sauce
pepper to taste

Ideal for freshwater fish
(lake trout, whitefish, pike, etc.)
with a bottle of McGregor
Keuka Highlands White.

Fillet fish, but do not scale or skin them. Cut in serving pieces or leave whole.

Prepare sauce by mixing ingredients and heating until blended. Place fish in glass dish and pour hot sauce over fish. Let marinate about an hour (if longer, put in refrigerator).

Start grill and lightly oil the rack. Place fish on hot grill, skin side down. Baste occasionally with sauce. When fish is easily separable from skin, carefully insert spatula between skin and meat and turn fish over onto the skin (the skin serves as a pan). Continue cooking and basting (use all the sauce) until fish flakes easily - about 10 minutes.

Per serving: 452 Calories; 19g Fat (41% calories from fat); 57g Protein; 4g Carbohydrate; 227mg Cholesterol; 350 mg Sodium

NOTES

_____

_____

_____

_____

_____

Cheryl's Scallops in Mustard Sauce

From Lemon Creek Winery, Michigan

Serves 8

1 1/2 cups dry white wine
1 1/2 cups clam juice
2 whole bay leaves
4 tablespoons Dijon mustard
1 cup whipping cream
1/2 cup clarified butter
2 pounds scallops
all-purpose flour
2 cloves garlic, minced
3/4 pound mushrooms, thickly sliced
2 tablespoons parsley, minced

Serve with your favorite green salad, over pasta or with crusty French bread and a glass of Lemon Creek Vignoles.

Combine in a saucepan: wine, clam juice and bay leaves. Bring to a boil. Add Dijon mustard and whipping cream, bring to a boil again. Reduce heat and simmer 30 minutes to 1 hour. Remove bay leaves. Cool.

Heat clarified butter (melted butter with salty foam removed and settled cream used) in a saute pan.

Dredge scallops in seasoned flour (salt and pepper or favorite prepared seasoning mix) and sear quickly to a light golden color. Add minced garlic and mustard sauce. Bring to a boil. Add mushrooms. Cook until the sauce is desired consistency.

Add parsley and serve immediately.

Per serving: 394 Calories; 26g Fat (63% calories from fat); 22g Protein; 12g Carbohydrate; 113mg Cholesterol; 478mg Sodium

NOTES

_____

_____

_____

Flamboyant Pacific Snapper

From Kittling Ridge Estate Wines & Spirits, Ontario

Serves 12

3 pounds fish fillets cut in 1" strips
1/2 cup flour
1/2 cup extra virgin olive oil
fresh ground pepper
2 medium onions, cut in thin slivers
6 tablespoons golden raisins
6 tablespoons dry white wine
3/4 cup pine nuts, toasted
1 1/2 cups dry white wine
6 tablespoons white wine vinegar
6 tablespoons honey

A unique fish variation
using Kittling Ridge
Sauvignon Blanc.

Place raisins in a small, microwave-safe dish with the 6 tablespoons of wine. Cover with plastic wrap. Microwave on high for 1 minute. Allow raisins to soak in the wine while continuing with the recipe.

In a plastic bag, toss the fish fillets (snapper, sole, orange roughy or halibut) with the flour.

In a large non-stick pan, heat 4 tablespoons of olive oil. Working in batches, saute the fillet pieces quickly, until golden. You will need to add more of the oil as you go along. Transfer each batch to a large shallow serving dish and liberally sprinkle with fresh ground pepper.

Heat the remaining olive oil in the same skillet. Saute onions for 8-10 minutes, but do not brown.

Scatter onions over the fish along with the raisins and pine nuts. Whisk together the vinegar, 1/2 cup of wine and the honey. Drizzle over the fish. Refrigerate for 3-4 hours or overnight. Do not cover until the mixture has chilled to prevent extra condensation. Bring to room temperature before serving.

Per serving: 308 Calories; 14g Fat (42% calories from fat); 23g Protein; 19g Carbohydrate; 49mg Cholesterol; 156mg Sodium

Goujonnettes of Lake Erie Walleye

From Chef Tom Johnson, Mon Ami Winery and Restaurant, Ohio

Serves 4

2 pounds walleye pike fillets
1 cup dry white wine
2 cups flour
1 teaspoon sea salt, coarse
1/2 teaspoon cayenne pepper
1/2 teaspoon mace, powdered
1/2 cup vegetable shortening
  or enough to fry
1 lemon, quartered

The Great Lakes version of this French delicacy uses walleye, whitefish, lake trout or bass and a bottle of Mon Ami Lake Erie Chardonnay.

Remove any tendon, fat or bone particles from the walleye fillets. Cut the fillets crosswise into strips about 1/4 inch by 4 inches long. Place the strips in a small glass bowl and cover with the wine.

Season the flour with sea salt, cayenne pepper and the mace. Remove the strips from the wine and dredge them in the seasoned flour.

Heat the vegetable oil in a wok, fry pan or electric skillet, to a temperature of 365 degrees F., measured by a quick-read or candy thermometer. Carefully place the floured fish strips into the hot fat. Fry for 6 to 8 minutes until the strips are golden brown. Carefully lift the "goujonettes" from the oil to drain on paper towels. Sprinkle with a bit of coarse salt. Turn onto a plate covered with a paper doily or a linen napkin. Garnish with lemon wedges and a sprinkle of snipped fresh parsley. Serve with RED ONION TARTAR SAUCE (see recipe).

Per serving: 716 Calories; 29g Fat (39% calories from fat); 50g Protein; 51g Carbohydrate; 210mg Cholesterol; 591mg Sodium

NOTES

_____

_____

_____

Grilled Fish

From Fenn Valley Vineyards, Michigan

Serves 4

2 pounds fish fillets firm for grilling
1/2 cup soy sauce
3/4 cup white wine, semi-dry
1 medium onion, finely diced
1 tablespoon lemon juice
1 1/2 tablespoons garlic, chopped
1 tablespoon ginger, chopped
1 medium orange juice and pulp
dash sesame oil

A recipe for your prize catch, then reward yourself with Fenn Valley Dry Riesling.

Mix all ingredients except fish in a large zip-lock baggie. Insert fish. Squeeze out air. Refrigerate for 2-5 hours.

Remove. Sprinkle lightly with paprika (optional). Grill 3 minutes on one side. Flip. Grill 2-3 minutes on second side. Baste cooked side with marinade. Flip and grill for 1 minute or until the fish is just cooked through. Be careful not to overcook!

Per serving: 260 Calories; 2g Fat (7% calories from fat); 43g Protein; 9g Carbohydrate; 98mg Cholesterol; 1920mg Sodium

NOTES

_____

_____

_____

_____

_____

_____

_____

Herb-Crusted Salmon

From Bowers Harbor Vineyards, Michigan

Serves 4

2 salmon fillets cut in serving sizes
3 tablespoons butter or margarine
1 cup bread crumbs or Drakes® mix
1/4 cup sun-dried tomatoes,
  finely chopped
1 teaspoon oregano
1 teaspoon thyme
1 teaspoon basil

A glass of Bowers Harbor Vineyards Riesling is an ideal companion for the cook in the kitchen as well as with the salmon at the dinner table.

Remove skin from salmon and marinate in a prepared Italian salad dressing. Refrigerate for several hours.

Combine crumbs, tomatoes and seasonings.

Shake off excess dressing from fish and dredge in coating mixture. Saute in butter or margarine over medium heat, turning once until golden brown and cooked.

Per serving: 296 Calories; 13g Fat (41% calories from fat); 21g Protein; 22g Carbohydrate; 67mg Cholesterol; 403mg Sodium

NOTES

_____

_____

_____

_____

_____

_____

Jambalaya, Lake Erie Style

From Chef Tom Johnson, Firelands Winery, Ohio

Serves 8

2 pounds shrimp, peeled & deveined
2 cups chicken stock
1 cup dry white wine
1 bay leaf
parsley stems
2 teaspoons sea salt
3 tablespoons butter
3 tablespoons bacon drippings, fresh
1 pound smoked ham cut in $^1/2$" cubes
2 red onions, finely chopped
1 teaspoon dried thyme
2 stalks celery with leaves, chopped
1 small green bell pepper, seeded & diced
1 cup short-grain rice
28 $^1/2$ ounces canned tomatoes, diced
3 tablespoons tomato paste
$^1/4$ pound okra, cut $^1/2$ inch thick
2 cloves garlic, peeled and minced
1 tablespoon Italian parsley, finely chopped
$^1/8$ teaspoon ground cloves
$^1/4$ teaspoon ground mace
2 jalapeno peppers, seeded and minced
$^1/4$ teaspoon fresh ground pepper

> This recipe is worth the effort, especially with a bottle of Fireland's Chardonnay at your side and on the dinner table.

Preheat oven to 350 degrees F.

Peel shrimp and place shells, chicken stock, wine, bay leaf and parsley stems into a non-reactive saucepan. Simmer gently for an hour. Then strain and reserve. There should be slightly more than 2 cups.

Melt the butter and the bacon dripping in a heavy 5 or 6-quart, oven-proof casserole. Briefly fry the ham pieces to evaporate the excess water that may be in the meat. Remove meat to a plate and reserve.

Add the onions and thyme to the fat and saute until the onions are turning transparent. Then, stir in the celery and the peppers and saute them for another minute or two. Stir in the rice, stirring to coat each grain with fat.

Stir until the rice is somewhat opaque and milky white. Add the tomatoes and tomato paste, blending well. Add the garlic, the okra, parsley, ground clove, ground mace, jalapeno pepper, black pepper and the chicken stock.

Cover and bake for 25 minutes. Remove from oven, stir in the ham and cover for another 15 minutes using only the heat from the casserole. Uncover and scatter the shrimps on top of the hot rice. Cover again and steam the shrimps in the pot, out of the oven, for an additional 15 minutes. Uncover and stir to blend well. If the jambalaya is slightly dry, loosen it with additional wine.

Per serving: 374 Calories; 12g Fat (31% calories from fat); 28g Protein; 33g Carbohydrate; 189mg Cholesterol; 1076mg Sodium

NOTES

_____

_____

_____

_____

_____

_____

_____

_____

_____

Luscious Lemony Scallops

From Cedar Springs Wines, Ontario

Serves 4

2 tablespoons olive oil
1 1/2 pounds scallops, cleaned & peeled
1 lemon quarter, sliced thin
1 clove garlic, minced fine
1 teaspoon black pepper, coarsely ground
1 teaspoon fresh parsley, finely chopped
1 tablespoon dry white wine
1 tablespoon butter
salt and pepper to taste

A perfect choice with this seafood dish would be Cedar Springs Semillon Chardonnay.

Allow olive oil to become extremely hot in frying pan over high heat. Add scallops and saute quickly. Add all other ingredients except parsley, white wine and butter.

Continue to saute. Add white wine and butter. Adjust seasonings. Add parsley.

Divide onto plates and serve immediately.

Accompany with a rice dish and freshly prepared vegetables.

Per serving: 245 Calories; 11g Fat (40% calories from fat); 29g Protein; 8g Carbohydrate; 64mg Cholesterol; 305mg Sodium

NOTES

_____

_____

_____

_____

_____

_____

Pan-Grilled Scampi in Chardonnay Sauce

From Chef Rob Szabo, Mon Ami Winery and Restaurant, Ohio

Serves 4

1/2 pint cherry tomatoes,
  quartered
3 cloves garlic, minced
2 ounces fresh basil, chopped
3 ounces extra virgin olive oil
2 pounds shrimp, peeled &
  deveined
2 cups Chardonnay
2 lemons, halved
salt to taste
fresh ground pepper

Spoon this recipe over rice, fresh spinach leaves or a pasta of your choice. Accompany with Mon Ami Lake Erie Chardonnay or Mon Ami Proprietor's Reserve Chardonnay.

Combine tomatoes, garlic and half the basil with about a third of the oil. Reserve.

Butterfly the shrimp (10-15 count) by cutting them, lengthwise, about half way through their center. Reserve.

Preheat a large saute pan, or a wok and add the remainder of the oil, listening for a pinging noise which will let you know that the oil is hot enough. Gently add the reserved shrimp, being careful of the hot oil popping as you are doing this. Quickly saute the shrimp for 1 to 2 minutes. Add the reserved tomato-garlic-basil mixture. Saute an additional 30 seconds. Add the wine, and over high heat, cook until the wine has reduced by two-thirds. Season to taste by squeezing the fresh lemon halves, and with salt and freshly ground black pepper.

Per serving: 534 Calories; 25g Fat (49% calories from fat); 48g Protein; 12g Carbohydrate; 345mg Cholesterol; 348mg Sodium

NOTES

_____

_____

Poached Lake Michigan Trout

From Leelanau Cellars, Michigan

Serves 8

6 pounds trout fresh whole, cleaned
1 large onion sliced
3 ribs celery with leaves
1/2 teaspoon salt
1/2 teaspoon pepper
1/2 cup dry white wine
1 lemon thinly sliced

Serve as an appetizer, entree or brunch dish with Leelanau Cellars Renaissance, Spring Splendor or Winter White.

Spread out a large piece of heavy duty aluminum foil. Using vegetable oil, lightly coat the skin of the fish before putting it on the foil. Salt and pepper the cavity and fill with onions and celery. Then pour in the dry white wine and carefully fold over the foil on the ends as well as the top so it doesn't leak.

Poach fish in a 325 degrees F. oven 10-12 minutes to the pound.

Remove from oven and open foil to cool. Pour off liquid and refrigerate.

When cold, remove the skin and transfer to an attractive platter. Garnish with thinly sliced lemons. Cherry tomatoes, parsley, cucumbers and slices of hard boiled eggs can be arranged around the fish. See GREEN FISH SAUCE in the Dips & Sauces section for an excellent accompaniment to this dish.

Per serving: 523 Calories; 23g Fat (41% calories from fat); 71g Protein; 3g Carbohydrate; 197mg Cholesterol; 392mg Sodium

NOTES

_____

_____

_____

_____

_____

Poached Salmon

From Lemon Creek Winery, Michigan

Serves 8

1 quart water
2 cups dry white wine, Vignoles
1 rib celery, chopped
1 carrot, chopped
1 medium onion, stuck with 2 cloves
1 clove garlic, halved
1 teaspoon salt
1 strip lemon peel
2 sprigs parsley
ground black pepper
5 pounds salmon with head & tail

Served on a hot platter with lemon wedges or your favorite fish sauce and a glass of Lemon Creek Dry Vignoles.

Combine all ingredients, except salmon, for preparation of a court bouillon in a fish poacher. Bring to a boil, reduce and simmer 15 minutes.

Place fish in the poacher and poach gently, 10 minutes for each inch of fish measured at its thickest point.

Remove fish immediately when it is flaky at the thickest point.

Per serving: 416 Calories; 10g Fat (25% calories from fat); 60g Protein; 10g Carbohydrate; 148mg Cholesterol; 538mg Sodium

NOTES

_____

_____

_____

_____

_____

_____

Prawn and Pancetta Skewers with Chive Sauce

From Chef Izabela Kalabis, Inniskillin Winery, Ontario

Serves 4

20 large shrimp, peeled &
  deveined
8 slices pancetta or bacon,
  cut in 1/2" strips
1 tablespoon butter

CHIVE SAUCE
2 shallots, minced
1/4 cup dry white wine
3/4 cup fish stock
1/2 cup cream
1 tablespoon fresh chives,
  finely chopped
3/4 cup cold butter
 salt and pepper

Look for authentic prawns and pancetta or use jumbo shrimp and high quality bacon for this recipe. Then serve a classic Inniskillin Chardonnay from the Niagara Peninsula.

Wrap each prawn with a slice of pancetta and thread 5 wrapped prawns onto each skewer. Set aside while preparing sauce.

CHIVE SAUCE
Place shallots and wine in a small pan. Cook to a glaze. Add stock and continue simmering until 2 tablespoons remain. Add cream, lower heat to minimum and whisk in butter a piece at a time. Take off heat, adjust seasoning. Add chives and place in hot waterbath to keep warm.

Heat 1 tablespoon of butter in a medium size frying pan and fry the skewers on both sides until pancetta is crisp and prawns are cooked, or about 2 minutes each side. Place one skewer on each serving plate with 1 tablespoon of sauce on the side.

Per serving: 505 Calories; 47g Fat (85% calories from fat); 15g Protein; 4g Carbohydrate; 228mg Cholesterol; 530mg Sodium

Meat

Barbecued Loin Pork Chops

From Reif Estate Winery, Ontario

Serves 4

4 pork chops
3 tablespoons seasoned flour
2 tablespoons olive oil
1/4 cup onion, chopped
1/4 cup celery, diced
2 tablespoons brown sugar
1 1/2 tablespoons lemon juice
1/2 teaspoon salt
1/8 teaspoon red pepper
1 tablespoon dry mustard
1/2 teaspoon chili powder
1/2 cup dry white wine, Riesling
1 cup tomato sauce

You'll enjoy a nice, cool glass of Reif Estate Dry Riesling wine with this tangy chop.

Coat chops in seasoned flour and brown in the oil. Place in ovenproof dish. Mix remaining ingredients together and pour over meat. Cover and bake at 350 degrees F. for one hour, basting occasionally.

Per serving: 357 Calories; 22g Fat (59% calories from fat); 24g Protein; 11g Carbohydrate; 74mg Cholesterol; 745mg Sodium

NOTES

_____

_____

_____

_____

_____

_____

Beef Stew Leelanau

From Leelanau Cellars, Michigan

Serves 6

1 1/2 pounds beef chuck, cubed
1 tablespoon shortening
1 clove garlic, minced
1 medium onion, chopped
1/2 teaspoon salt
1/4 teaspoon pepper
1 can tomato soup, undiluted
1/4 cup water
3/4 cup dry red wine, Baco Noir
1/4 teaspoon basil
1/4 teaspoon thyme
3 medium carrots, sliced
1 1/2 cups celery, sliced
4 medium potatoes, pared and sliced

"A Taste of Northern Michigan" and served with Leelanau Cellars Autumn Harvest or Baco Noir.

Brown beef in shortening. Add garlic and onions and saute until tender. Add salt and pepper.

Stir in tomato soup, water and dry red wine. Cover; simmer 30 minutes.

Add basil, thyme and vegetables. Cover; simmer for 2 hours or until tender.

Like a good soup, this stew can be made the day before.

Per serving: 356 Calories; 20g Fat (54% calories from fat); 20g Protein; 18g Carbohydrate; 66mg Cholesterol; 496mg Sodium

NOTES

_____

_____

_____

_____

Choucroute Garnie

From Glenora Wine Cellars, Finger Lakes, New York

Serves 6

2 pounds sauerkraut
3 medium onions
2 tablespoons bacon fat
2 medium tart apples, peeled,
  cored and sliced
6 peppercorns
10 juniper berries or 1/4 cup of gin
2 1/2 cups Riesling wine
12 sausage links
6 slices cooked ham sliced 1/4" thick
6 pork chops, smoked
6 frankfurters

An Alsatian dish especially nice for winter parties since it can be made ahead. Serve with plenty of Glenora Wine Cellars Johannisberg Riesling.

Soak sauerkraut in cold water for 15 minutes. Squeeze dry. Meanwhile, saute onions in fat until tender. Add sauerkraut and toss with fork. Cook for 5 minutes, stirring occasionally. Add apples, peppercorns and juniper berries. Pour in Riesling. Cook slowly, covered, for 1 hour.

Fry sausages. Drain off fat and put sausages on absorbent paper. Cook, covered, for 30 minutes longer. Discard peppercorns and juniper berries.

To serve, spoon out meats onto plate. Pile sausages in center of large warm platter. Arrange meats and sausages on platter and cover with sauerkraut. Serve with boiled potatoes and mustard.

Per serving: 1070 Calories; 74g Fat (66% calories from fat); 64g Protein; 21g Carbohydrate; 225mg Cholesterol; 4221mg Sodium

NOTES

_____

_____

_____

_____

Country Veal

From Leelanau Cellars, Michigan

Serves 4

1 1/2 pounds veal steak, top round
flour
1 1/2 tablespoons vegetable oil
1/2 teaspoon salt
1/8 teaspoon pepper
1/2 teaspoon garlic salt
1/2 teaspoon paprika
1/2 teaspoon dry mustard
1/4 teaspoon Worcestershire sauce
1/8 teaspoon dried rosemary
1 tablespoon catsup
1/2 cup semi-dry white wine
1/2 cup sour cream
1 medium tomato, quartered
parsley for garnish

"A Taste of Northern Michigan" served with Leelanau Cellars Spring Splendor or Winter White.

Cut veal into serving size pieces. Dredge with flour and brown on both sides in heated oil.

Combine salt, pepper, garlic salt, paprika, mustard, Worcestershire, rosemary, catsup and semi-dry white wine. Stir until blended.

Pour over browned veal. Cover and simmer until tender, about 40-50 minutes.

Remove to platter, keep hot. Add sour cream to drippings left in pan and heat but do not boil.

Pour over meat. Garnish with parsley and quartered tomato.

Per serving: 296 Calories; 19g Fat (57% calories from fat); 27g Protein; 4g Carbohydrate; 123mg Cholesterol; 447mg Sodium

NOTES

_____

_____

_____

_____

Dutch Apple Pork Chops

From Heritage Wine Cellars, Pennsylvania

Serves 6

6 pork chops, lean
2 medium onions. sliced
1 cup mushrooms, sliced
1 tablespoon olive oil
1 tablespoon brown sugar
1 tablespoon garlic powder
1/2 cup apple wine
1/2 cup orange juice

A black iron skillet, like grandma used, works best for this recipe. And don't forget the Heritage Dutch Apple wine.

In skillet pour olive oil and add pork chops. Mix juice, wine, brown sugar and garlic powder. Pour over pork chops. Arrange sliced onions and mushrooms on top of meat. Cover the skillet. Cook over medium heat.

Check when meat is poached, turn over carefully and lightly brown otherside, placing onions and mushrooms on a warmed serving platter.

This dish is good with mashed potato-herbed dumplings and cooked greens. May also consider brown rice and steamed honey carrots.

Per serving: 283 Calories; 17g Fat (55% calories from fat); 24g Protein; 7g Carbohydrate; 74mg Cholesterol; 243mg Sodium

NOTES

_____

_____

_____

_____

_____

_____

_____

Escalope of Veal Vidal

From Ferrante Winery & Ristorante, Ohio

Serves 6

3 pounds veal cutlet or medallions
1 1/2 cups semi-dry white wine
1 cup fresh mushrooms, sliced
1/2 cup corn syrup white
1 tablespoon pepper
1/8 cup flour
4 ounces olive oil
2 ounces butter

An elegant meat course beautifully complemented with a glass of Ferrante Vidal Blanc.

Dredge veal in flour.

Heat olive oil in large saucepan and saute veal until brown (4-5 minutes).

Add mushrooms and pepper. Cook for 2 minutes. Add wine and syrup and continue cooking for 3 minutes.

Per serving: 574 Calories; 32g Fat (51% calories from fat); 47g Protein; 24g Carbohydrate; 211mg Cholesterol; 301mg Sodium

NOTES

_____

_____

_____

_____

_____

_____

_____

_____

Ham Steak with Class

From von Stiehl Winery, Wisconsin

Serves 6

2 tablespoons butter
2 tablespoons sugar
dash ground ginger
2 pounds ham steak, cut 1 1/2 inch thick
1 tablespoon onion, finely chopped
3/4 cup dry cherry wine
1 tablespoon cornstarch
1/4 cup cold water
1 cup seedless grapes, green

Ham and von Stiehl Dry Cherry wine are naturals for holiday presentations.

Melt butter in large skillet. Sprinkle in sugar and ginger. Brown ham quickly on both sides in mixture. Remove ham.

Cook onions in drippings until tender. Blend in the wine, cook and stir until boiling. Combine cornstarch and cold water. Add to wine mixture.

Halve grapes. Add to sauce and cook 1 to 2 minutes more. Spoon grapes and sauce over ham on warm platter and serve.

Per serving: 256 Calories; 10g Fat (37% calories from fat); 30g Protein; 10g Carbohydrate; 78mg Cholesterol; 1968mg Sodium

NOTES

_____

_____

_____

_____

_____

_____

_____

Hot 'n' Sweet Barbecue

From Arbor Hill Grapery, Finger Lakes, New York

Serves 10

12 ounces Sherried Wine Barbecue Sauce
  * see note
1 cup raspberry jam or
  Concord grape jam
1/2 medium onion, finely chopped
2 teaspoons hot pepper sauce to taste
5 pounds pork spareribs
2 pounds skinless boneless chicken
  breast halves

A tasty barbecue complemented by your favorite Great Lakes Chancellor wine.

In medium bowl, combine barbecue sauce, jam, onion and pepper sauce. Set aside.

Cut ribs into 3-rib portions. Lightly brush both sides of ribs with sauce mixture. Place meaty side down in 13x9x2-inch glass baking dish. Cover with waxed paper and microwave on medium for 25 minutes. (Or heat in oven at 375 degrees F., covered with foil, for 20 minutes on each side).

Prepare and heat outdoor grill.

Place ribs and chicken on grill rack 5 inches from heat. Grill 10-15 minutes, turning and brushing often with barbecue sauce.

Brush on extra sauce before serving. Heat and serve remaining sauce in small bowl.

*Arbor Hill Sherried Wine Barbecue Sauce is available by catalog directly from the Grapery (see the winery listing).

Per serving: 585 Calories; 35g Fat (54% calories from fat); 45g Protein; 21g Carbohydrate; 162mg Cholesterol; 209mg Sodium

NOTES

_____

_____

_____

_____

Italian Stuffed Steak

From Fenn Valley Vineyards, Michigan

Serves 4

2 pounds beef steak
1 cup dry red wine
3/8 cup bread crumbs
3/8 cup parsley, minced
3 tablespoons Parmesan cheese, grated
3 tablespoons capers
1 1/2 tablespoons pine nuts, toasted
6 cloves garlic, minced
3/4 teaspoon rosemary, ground

Yes, it may be red meat, but try this dish with Fenn Valley Pinot Gris.

Put the red wine in a small pan and reduce over high heat to 2 tablespoons. Prepare the stuffing by combining the reduced red wine with all ingredients except meat in a bowl, stir well, set aside. Add additional non-reduced red wine if needed to give the stuffing a pasty consistency.

Trim any fat from the steak. Cut horizontally through the center of the steak to open like a butterfly. Place steak between two plastic sheets and hammer to an even 1/4" thickness with a meat mallet.

Spread above mixture over steak to within 1/2 inch of the outside edges. Roll up in a jelly roll fashion and tie with cotton string at 2" intervals (when using oven) or pin with toothpicks at 3/4" intervals (for grilling).

Oven: Bake at 350 degrees F. for 25-30 minutes. Cut into 8-10 slices.

Grilling: Place on a hot grill and cook until the outside is lightly browned and the meat is firm. Slice into 1 1/2 inch thick slices. Continue grilling pieces on a hot fire until cooked through.

Per serving: 637 Calories; 43g Fat (66% calories from fat); 38g Protein; 13g Carbohydrate; 130mg Cholesterol; 318mg Sodium

NOTES

_____

_____

_____

Joe's Italian Meatballs

From Joe Borrello

Serves 16

1 pound ground chuck
1/2 pound Italian sausage ground bulk
1 medium yellow onion, finely chopped
3 cloves garlic, finely chopped
2 teaspoons fresh parsley, finely chopped
1 egg
1 cup bread crumbs, Progresso® seasoned
1/2 cup milk or milk/red wine
2/3 cup Parmesan cheese, grated
salt and pepper to taste

A tasty accompaniment cooked in "Old World" Spaghetti Sauce and a glass of Great Lakes Chancellor or Foch red wine.

Mix all ingredients well and form into medium size balls. Place directly in sauce and allow to simmer for 1-2 hours. Let sit in sauce overnight and simmer for additional 2-3 hours before serving. Freeze leftovers in sauce.

Per serving: 178 Calories; 12g Fat (63% calories from fat); 10g Protein; 6g Carbohydrate; 47mg Cholesterol; 240mg Sodium

NOTES

_____

_____

_____

_____

_____

_____

_____

_____

Klauses Lamb in Chardonnay

From Reif Estate Winery, Ontario

Serves 6

2 pounds lamb, cubed
salt and pepper to taste
flour
3 tablespoons olive oil
2 cloves garlic, crushed
1 1/2 cups Chardonnay
6 green peppers, chopped
1 large tomato, chopped
1/4 cup onion, chopped
1/2 tablespoon rosemary
1 bay leaf

Reif Estate Chardonnay is a good choice for this recipe, as an ingredient as well as on the table when it is served.

Sprinkle bite-sized pieces of lamb with salt and pepper and dust with flour. In skillet, add oil, crushed garlic, onions and meat; fry until lightly browned, stirring frequently. Add Chardonnay wine until liquid is reduced to 1/3. Add peppers, tomatoes, bay leaf and rosemary to lamb. Cover and simmer for 3/4 hour. Serve warm over a bed of rice.

Per serving: 327 Calories; 15g Fat (47% calories from fat); 31g Protein; 6g Carbohydrate; 98mg Cholesterol; 129mg Sodium

NOTES

_____

_____

_____

_____

_____

Maple Mustard Chops

From Kittling Ridge Estate Wines & Spirits, Ontario

Serves 4

4 pork chops, 1/2 inch thick
1 teaspoon vegetable oil
1/4 cup Maple Brandy Liqueur
  * see note
1 teaspoon Dijon mustard

Kittling Ridge Maple Brandy Liqueur gives this dish its special flavor, but apple brandy or Calvados may be used as a substitute.

    Brown chops in oil, cover and cook. Remove chops, drain fat. Add Maple Liqueur and mustard to a pan and whisk. Pour over chops and simmer 2 minutes per side. Serve with a side of rice, pasta or roasted potatoes.

    *Maple Brandy Liqueur is available at Liqour Control Board of Ontario (LCBO) retail stores or from the Kittling Ridge Retail Store (see winery listings).

Per serving: 243 Calories; 16g Fat (61% calories from fat); 23g Protein; 0g Carbohydrate; 74mg Cholesterol; 74mg Sodium

NOTES

_____

_____

_____

_____

_____

_____

_____

_____

Mother's Stew with a Twist

From L. Mawby Vineyards, Michigan

Serves 6

1 pound lean beef, cut 1 inch cubes
4 tablespoons butter
4 cloves garlic, minced
4 medium onions, diced
1 cup water
2 cups dry red wine
3 tablespoons bacon grease
4 carrots, sliced
6 medium potatoes, cubed
4 stalks celery, sliced
1 large onion, chopped
salt and pepper to taste
1/2 cup fresh parsley, chopped

Accompany this stew with homemade bread and butter plus a glass of L. Mawby Turkey Red Wine.

Fry beef in butter with garlic and diced onions until dry. Add and fry out, one cup at a time, the water and wine. Add and melt the bacon grease. Add enough water to cover meat by 1 inch. Add vegetables, salt, pepper and parsley. Simmer until vegetables are just tender.

Per serving: 404 Calories; 18g Fat (46% calories from fat); 21g Protein; 27g Carbohydrate; 71mg Cholesterol; 662mg Sodium

NOTES

_____

_____

_____

_____

_____

_____

Mrs. C's Classic Pork Loin Chops

From Casa Larga Vineyards, Finger Lakes, New York

Serves 4

4 pork loin chops
1 1/4 cups bread crumbs, plain
1 cup balsamic vinegar
1 cup extra virgin olive oil
2 cups champagne
2 large plum tomatoes, ripened,
    peeled and seeded, coarsely chopped
1 clove garlic, finely chopped
salt and pepper to taste

Serve with baked potato, tossed salad, warm Italian bread and a bottle of Casa Larga Petite Noir to complete a wonderful meal.

Preheat oven to 400 degrees F. Lightly grease bottom of a deep oven pan.

Place bread crumbs in plastic bag with pork chops and shake until chops are completely covered. Place chops in pan and spread tomatoes over top, sprinkle salt and pepper to taste. Add 1/4 of each liquid ingredient (balsamic vinegar, oil and champagne). Cover with wax paper first and then with aluminum foil. Bake for ten minutes.

Add 1/4 more of the liquid ingredients, cover and bake another 10 minutes. Repeat this procedure two more times, finishing all the liquid (the secret is to keep the chops moist while baking).

Turn broiler on and brown for 5 to 10 minutes. Remove from oven and spread garlic and parsley over the top, salt and pepper to taste, serve with the remaining juices over the chops.

Per serving: 956 Calories; 71g Fat (73% calories from fat); 27g Protein; 32g Carbohydrate; 74mg Cholesterol; 295mg Sodium

NOTES

Orange Beef Stir-Fry

From Cedar Springs Wines, Ontario

Serves 6

1/4 cup soy sauce
1/2 cup orange juice
1/4 teaspoon ground ginger
1/4 teaspoon garlic powder
16 ounces beef roast, cooked
   strip cuts
2 tablespoons cooking oil
1 medium red onion sliced
2 cups snow peas
1 cup fresh mushrooms, sliced
1 medium green pepper, sliced
10 ounces mandarin oranges,
   drained
2 tablespoons cornstarch

This tasty and colorful stir-fry is a great way to use leftover roast beef. An ideal accompaniment is the earthy, rich taste of Cedar Springs Cuvee Reserve Red Wine.

    Combine soy sauce, orange juice, ginger and garlic; pour over beef strips. Set aside. Heat oil in wok or frypan. Add vegetables. Cook uncovered for 2 minutes. Lift beef from marinade. Add beef strips and orange segments to vegetables.
    Combine reserved marinade with cornstarch; add to wok.
    Heat, just to thicken. Serve immediately over rice.

Per serving: 274 Calories; 17g Fat (55% calories from fat); 15g Protein; 16g Carbohydrate; 44mg Cholesterol; 711mg Sodium

NOTES

_____

_____

_____

_____

_____

Roast Venison with Morels

From Lemon Creek Winery, Michigan

Serves 6

2 tablespoons olive oil
3 pounds venison
1 medium onion, chopped
1 carrot, chopped
4 cups water
2 cups dry red wine
2 cups beef broth, canned
2 whole bay leaves
1 sprig thyme, fresh
1 clove garlic, minced
6 juniper berrries
6 whole peppercorns
6 tablespoons butter
1 pound morels, stemmed and sliced
6 slices bacon

> Specially prepared for the deer and mushroom hunters while being served a glass of Lemon Creek Chambourcin.

Heat oil in a large, heavy Dutch oven over medium heat. Add onion and carrot; saute 15 minutes.

Add water, wine, broth, bay leaves, thyme, garlic, juniper berries and peppercorns. Bring to boil. Reduce heat to medium-low. Simmer 1 1/2 hours, skimming ocasionally. Strain into a medium saucepan and boil until reduced to 3/4 cup, about 30 minutes. Season with salt and pepper.

Preheat oven to 375 degrees F. Wrap bacon strips around roast and secure with toothpicks. Roast in a roasting pan or heavy skillet, 1/2 hour per pound (1 1/2 hours for a 3 pound roast). When done, transfer to platter and cover with foil.

Melt 2 tablespoons butter in the same pan and saute morels until tender, about 5 minutes. Season with salt and pepper.

Bring sauce to simmer. Remove from heat and add remaining 4 tablespoons of butter, 1 tablespoon at a time, whisking until just melted.

Remove the bacon strips from the venison and slice. Serve with the morels and sauce.

Per serving: 719 Calories; 34g Fat (46% calories from fat); 76g Protein; 13g Carbohydrate; 223mg Cholesterol; 1839mg Sodium

Sherried Flank Steak

From Arbor Hill Grapery, Finger Lakes, New York

Serves 12

1 cup Sherried Wine Barbecue Sauce
  * see note
1/2 teaspoon dried basil
1/2 teaspoon dried marjoram
1/4 teaspoon dried oregano
3 pounds flank steak
1/4 teaspoon fresh ground pepper

Great recipe for the grill chef, especially when using Arbor Hill Grapery wine sauces.

Combine barbecue sauce, basil, marjoram and oregano in gallon-size plastic food storage bag. Add steaks. Refrigerate 24 hours, turning occasionally.

Remove steaks, reserve marinade.

Grill steaks 5 to 6 inches over medium-hot coals for 5 minutes. Brush with marinade, turn and grill 5 to 8 minutes or until cooked to desired doneness.

Remove steaks. Sprinkle with pepper. Let stand 5 minutes. Diagonally cut across grain into thin slices.

Serve with your favorite vegetable and potato, rice or tube pasta recipes.

*Arbor Hill Sherried Wine Barbecue Sauce is available by catalog directly from the Grapery (see the winery listing).

Per serving: 201 Calories; 12g Fat (55% calories from fat); 22g Protein; 0g Carbohydrate; 58mg Cholesterol; 79mg Sodium

NOTES

_____

_____

_____

_____

_____

_____

Special Meat Loaf

From L. Mawby Vineyards, Michigan

Serves 12

3 pounds lean ground beef
1 large onion, coarsely chopped
1 large green bell pepper, chopped
2 medium eggs
3 tablespoons parsley
3 tablespoons Parmesan cheese
1/2 teaspoon basil
1 teaspoon herbal salt substitute
1/4 teaspoon garlic powder
1/4 teaspoon onion powder
1 cup oatmeal
1/2 cup wheat bran
1 cup dry red wine

A Great Lakes country twist to this basic entree. L. Mawby Foch is the perfect companion.

Combine ingredients, mixing well. Bake in two ungreased loaf pans at 375 degrees F. for 1 1/2 hours. Freeze leftovers.

Per serving: 367 Calories; 25g Fat (64% calories from fat); 23g Protein; 8g Carbohydrate; 116mg Cholesterol; 230mg Sodium

NOTES

_____

_____

_____

_____

_____

_____

_____

Stuffed Pork Tenderloin

From Fenn Valley Vineyards, Michigan

Serves 4

2 pounds pork tenderloin
1/2 medium onion, chopped
1 stalk celery, chopped
1/2 cup dried cherries
1/4 cup walnuts, chopped
4 teaspoons parsley, finely chopped
1/4 cup dried bread crumbs
1/4 cup nonfat Ricotta cheese
1/2 package Egg Beaters® 99%
  egg substitute
3/4 teaspoon marjoram, dried
1/8 teaspoon allspice
1/4 cup port wine

On the grill in the summer or in the oven during the cold months, this dish deserves a glass of Fenn Valley Pinot Gris or Chardonel.

Saute onion and celery for 5 minutes in a non-stick pan sprayed with olive oil. Add cherries, walnuts and parsley and continue to cook for 3 minutes. Remove the onion, cherry and walnut mixture from the heat and allow to cool slightly. Meanwhile, mix remaining ingredients in a large bowl. Add the onion cherry mix to the large bowl and stir together well. Add more wine if the mixture is too dry.

Butterfly slice the tenderloin (or breast). Cover with plastic wrap and pound until about 1/4 inch thick. Brush inside surface lightly with olive oil and spread the stuffing mixture over the meat, leaving a 1/2 inch border along the outside edges of the meat. Roll the meat up and pin together with toothpicks.

Lightly brush the outside with olive oil.

In the oven: Bake at 350 degrees F. for 25-30 minutes.

On a hot grill: Cook the outside until lightly browned and the meat is firm. Slice into 1 1/2 inch thick slices and finish cooking pieces on the grill.

Per serving: 333 Calories; 9g Fat (26% calories from fat); 52g Protein; 5g Carbohydrate; 150mg Cholesterol; 248mg Sodium

Sweet and Sour Rabbit

From Warner Vineyards, Michigan

Serves 4

3 pounds rabbit, cut into pieces
2 tablespoons butter
2 tablespoons salt
2 teaspoons fresh ground black pepper
2 tablespoons whole juniper
  berries, crushed
1 carrot, chopped
1 medium onion, sliced
3 slices bacon, diced
1 cup cider vinegar
1 cup dry white, wine
1 tablespoon sugar
3 tablespoons flour
1/2 cup sour cream
3 ginger snaps, crumbled

Either Warner Chardonnay or Chancellor will complement this rabbit entree.

After washing the rabbit in cold running water, remove all excess skin and the covering over the muscles and wash again, then dry on paper towels. Put pieces into a large deep-dish glass or stainless steel bowl (not aluminum). Marinate with the mixture of vinegar, wine, salt, pepper, onion, carrot, juniper berries and 2 cups of water. Pour enough over the rabbit to cover all the pieces and refrigerate for 3 days, turning all the pieces each day. Remove the rabbit and dry on paper towels. Keep the marinade and strain out two cups. Cook bacon until transparent, add butter and rabbit in Dutch oven.

Brown rabbit pieces on all sides in the hot fat. Add one cup of marinade, simmer covered over low heat for one hour. Sprinkle sugar and flour over rabbit and gradually stir in another cup of marinade and the gingersnaps. Simmer for 20 minutes, stirring often. Then stir in the sour cream, simmer for 10 minutes. Serve with hot buttered noodles sprinkled with caraway seeds.

Per serving: 724 Calories; 34g Fat (45% calories from fat); 72g Protein; 21g Carbohydrate; 226mg Cholesterol; 3664mg Sodium

Tournedoes Madere (Sauteed Steak Filet with Madeira Glaze)

From Chef Tom Johnson, Lonz Winery, Ohio

Serves 4

16 ounces beef tenderloin,
   4 medallions @ 4 oz.
4 tablespoons unsalted butter
1 tablespoon vegetable oil
salt and pepper, freshly ground
1 shallot or white of 2 green onions,
   finely minced
4 ounces mushrooms, sliced
1 cup Madeira
1 tablespoon heavy cream

Very French and very easy... also a terrific way to glorify hamburger patties! Lonz 3-Islands Madeira is the wine of choice.

Melt 2 tablespoons of butter and add the vegetable oil to a saute pan over medium high heat. When the butter has stopped sizzling and is very hot, add the steaks and brown for 1 minute, then turn and brown the other side for one minute. Lower the heat and continue to saute for an additional minute on each side for rare, 2 minutes more each side for medium rare and 3 for medium. Remove the steaks to a heated platter. Sprinkle them with salt and freshly ground black pepper.

Pour any remaining fat out of the pan. Replace it with two tablespoons fresh butter. When the butter is sizzling, remove the pan from the fire and add the minced shallot or green onions. When they are lightly sauteed, add the mushroom slices and return the pan to the heat. Stir the mushrooms over medium heat until they yield their juices. Add the Madeira, increasing heat and scraping any meat juice particles into the liquid. Reduce the sauce to about 1/4 cup. Whisk in heavy cream. Spoon one tablespoon of sauce over each medallion.

Per serving: 564 Calories; 43g Fat (79% calories from fat); 21g Protein; 5g Carbohydrate; 118mg Cholesterol; 75mg Sodium

Veal Medallions with Herbs and Cream Sauce

From Linda Thom, Chateau des Charmes, Ontario

Serves 6

1/2 pound fresh mushrooms, cleaned and sliced
2 pounds veal medallions
2 tablespoons butter
2 tablespoons cooking oil
salt and pepper to taste
3/4 cup dry white wine
1/3 cup whipping cream
1 tablespoon chives, chopped
1 tablespoon parsley, chopped
1 tablespoon chervil, chopped
1 teaspoon tarragon, optional

Linda Thom is an Olympic gold medal winner in shooting and an accomplished cook. She cooks and serves this dish with Chateau des Charmes Chardonnay.

Saute mushrooms in hot butter. Remove to heated dish.

Fry the meat for 30 seconds on each side in hot oil and butter. Season the cooked side with salt and pepper. Remove to heated, buttered, ovenproof platter. Season the second side. Keep warm.

Degrease the pan and deglaze with the wine. Add cream and half of the fresh herbs. Reduce sauce by half. Meanwhile, arrange sauteed mushrooms over the meat.

(Note: May be prepared ahead of time up to this point. Cover with foil).

When ready to serve, drain fat and juice from meat. Pour sauce over all, cover with foil and place in the oven at 350 degrees F. for 15 minutes.

Remove foil and slip quickly under the broiler until brown. Sprinkle remaining fresh herbs over the top and serve immediately.

Per serving: 152 Calories; 13g Fat (87% calories from fat); 1g Protein; 3g Carbohydrate; 28mg Cholesterol; 50mg Sodium

NOTES

_____

_____

Veal Medallions with Wild Mushrooms

From Chef Izabela Kalabis, Inniskillin Winery, Ontario

Serves 4

2 pounds veal medallions from the fillet
2 tablespoons all-purpose flour
salt and pepper to taste
2 tablespoons clarified butter
1/3 cup dry white wine
1/4 cup veal stock (or chicken stock)
3 tablespoons butter
2 cups wild mushrooms, washed, coarsely chopped
1 tablespoon butter
salt and pepper
1 shallot, finely chopped
1 bunch flat leaf parsley, finely chopped

A tasty dish with Inniskillin Niagara Peninsula Pinot Noir.

Over moderately high heat, melt two tablespoons of butter. When it becomes golden in color add the veal medallions which have been seasoned with salt and pepper and lightly dredged in flour. Brown the medallions on each side. Take off heat. Remove medallions from pan and wrap in foil.

Deglaze pan with the wine, reduce liquid until one tablespoon remains. Add stock, reduce again, lower heat and mix in three tablespoons of butter. Season with salt and pepper. Set aside.

Melt one tablespoon of butter in a pan. When it sizzles, add the shallot, soften until transparent, add mushrooms, salt and pepper and saute for approximately three minutes.

Just before removing from heat add parsley. Transfer the medallions to serving plates, add and remaining juices to sauce. Coat medallions with sauce and serve with the mushrooms.

Per serving: 192 Calories; 18g Fat (89% calories from fat); 1g Protein; 4g Carbohydrate; 48mg Cholesterol; 190mg Sodium

Veal Shanks Great Lakes Style

From Michigan Vintner Wine Co., Michigan

Serves 6

3 pounds veal shank
white pepper, cracked
8 tablespoons unsalted butter, melted
2 tablespoons flour
1 medium onion, diced
2 carrots, diced
1 cup celery, chopped
8 cloves garlic, peeled & crushed
1/4 cup fresh parsley, chopped
1 bay leaf
1/4 teaspoon thyme
1/2 teaspoon tarragon
2 cups Riesling wine
1 1/2 cups chicken stock
1 tablespoon tomato paste
30 ounces white hominy, canned, drained & heated

An excellent "stick-to-your-ribs" Great Lakes meal with Michigan Vintner Riesling.

Sprinkle white pepper on veal to taste. Pour 4 tablespoons of melted butter over veal in ovenproof baking dish and cook in 400 degrees F. oven until golden brown (about 15-20 minutes). Lower oven temperature to 350 degrees F. and add vegetables and spices to veal dish. Bake for another 20 minutes, until golden brown. Add the wine to the veal and vegetables, cover and cook for another 30 minutes.

In a small saucepan, melt the other 4 tablespoons of butter and stir in flour, heating until a nut brown roux is formed. Add stock and tomato paste to the roux, blend thoroughly and add to the veal and vegetables cooking for another 30 minutes. Arrange each veal shank on a fluffy white bed of hominy and pour strained, thickened sauce over all (discard vegetables).

Per serving: 610 Calories; 25g Fat (41% calories from fat); 52g Protein; 29g Carbohydrate; 221mg Cholesterol; 759mg Sodium

Venison or Beef Roast in Wine Sauce

From Frontenac Point Vineyard, Finger Lakes, New York

Serves 6

4 pounds round roast, trimmed, venison or beef
4 cloves garlic, peeled and crushed
1 medium onion, cut in quarters
4 carrots, halved, sliced lengthwise
1 cup dry red wine
salt and pepper to taste

This is a flexible recipe which allows you to increase or add ingredients to your own taste, but don't forget the Frontenac Point Proprietor's Reserve red wine.

In a bowl, combine the wine, salt, pepper, crushed garlic and raw roast. Marinate for 1-2 hours. Put roast and onion into pot, pour marinade over, cover and simmer for about 2 hours (depending on size of roast and cut of meat). Add carrots and cook for about 20-30 minutes more. Remove roast from pot, slice, arrange cooked carrots around meat. Keep warm on platter. Bring marinade to a boil, thicken and serve as a sauce separately.

Per serving: 453 Calories; 15g Fat (32% calories from fat); 67g Protein; 2g Carbohydrate; 176mg Cholesterol; 266mg Sodium

NOTES

_____

_____

_____

_____

_____

_____

_____

Venison Swiss Steak

From Good Harbor Vineyards, Michigan

Serves 4

2 pounds venison, steak or cubes
2 1/2 ounces onion soup mix, dry package
2 cups dry red wine
16 ounces tomato sauce, canned
2 bay leaves
2 teaspoons Italian seasoning
    (basil, oregano etc)
1/2 cup flour for dredging
1/4 cup vegetable oil
salt and pepper to taste

A hearty hunter's dish served with potatoes, rice or spaetzle and a glass of Good Harbor Coastal red wine.

Pound venison on both sides with a meat mallet or cut into 1/2 inch cubes. Dredge meat in flour, then brown on both sides in hot oil. Drain.

Combine wine, tomato sauce, soup mix and seasonings and pour over meat in a high-edge saute or fry pan.

Bring mixture to a boil, reduce heat and simmer covered until tender (about 1 1/2 hours). Add more wine and water if sauce gets too thick.

Per serving: 762 Calories; 29g Fat (38% calories from fat); 73g Protein; 33g Carbohydrate; 187mg Cholesterol; 3270mg Sodium

NOTES

Wine, Herb & Garlic-Marinated Leg of Lamb

From Good Harbor Vineyards, Michigan

Serves 8

1/2 cup olive oil
1 medium onion, sliced
4 cloves garlic, minced
3 teaspoons Dijon mustard
2 tablespoons dried rosemary
1 cup dry white wine
1/3 cup lemon juice
1/2 teaspoon salt
1/2 teaspoon pepper
1/2 teaspoon red pepper flakes
1 leg of lamb, boned & butterflied

A bottle of Good Harbor Vignoles is always a guest-pleaser with this entree.

Bone, butterfly and cut off all fat/tallow from the leg of lamb.

Combine all ingredients (except lamb). Place the lamb in a large roasting pan and cover with the marinade mixture. Refrigerate overnight and turn several times.

Cook lamb over hot coals or on a gas grill, 15 minutes per side. Baste with marinade. When meat is done, let stand for 10 minutes and then slice for serving.

Per serving: 255 Calories; 21g Fat (81% calories from fat); 8g Protein; 3g Carbohydrate; 31mg Cholesterol; 253mg Sodium

NOTES

Pasta, Rice
& Potatoes

A Different Pesto

From Lucas Vineyards, Finger Lakes, New York

Serves 10

1/2 cup parsley
1 1/2 cups fresh basil
14 cloves garlic (yes, 14!)
1 cup olive oil
1/2 cup Riesling wine
1/4 cup pine nuts
pinch salt

A special pasta dish with a glass of Lucas Vineyards Riesling.

Place parsley, basil and garlic cloves in a food processor fitted with a steel blade. Turn on processor and add olive oil in a steady stream through the feed tube.

Add wine, pine nuts and salt; process until smooth. Makes 1 1/2 cups of pesto.

Toss with favorite pasta.

Per serving: 230 Calories; 23g Fat (91% calories from fat); 2g Protein; 3g Carbohydrate; 0mg Cholesterol; 15mg Sodium

NOTES

_____

_____

_____

_____

_____

_____

_____

_____

Fettuccine Quattro Fromagi

From Joe Borrello

Serves 4

1/2 pound spinach pasta,
  fresh or dried
1 tablespoon butter
1/4 cup dry white wine
1/4 cup havarti cheese, grated
1/4 cup farmer's cheese, grated
1/4 cup blue cheese, crumbled
1/4 cup Parmesan cheese
1/2 cup half and half
fresh ground pepper to taste

As the main entree, this recipe can be embellished with any combination of pine nuts, fresh mushrooms, peas, chopped chicken, veal strips and, of course, a glass of Great Lakes white wine.

Saute cooked pasta noodles in the butter and white wine. Add the havarte, farmer's, blue and Parmesan cheeses and stir only until melted and blended under medium high heat. Pour in the half and half and add ground black pepper, continue stirring until thick.

Serve immediately because it cools quickly.

Per serving: 166 Calories; 13g Fat (74% calories from fat); 8g Protein; 2g Carbohydrate; 39mg Cholesterol; 322mg Sodium

NOTES

_____

_____

_____

_____

_____

_____

_____

 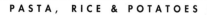

Gorgonzola Risotto with Grilled Chicken and Portabellos

From Joe Borrello

Serves 8

1 1/2 pounds skinless boneless chicken breast, grilled
8 ounces portabello mushrooms, grilled
8 ounces prepared Caesar salad dressing
1 1/2 cups Arborio rice
3 cups chicken stock
1/2 cup dry white wine
4 cloves garlic
1 bunch green onions, chopped
3 tablespoons extra virgin olive oil
1 cup peas, frozen or fresh
1 tablespoon fresh basil, finely chopped
1/2 teaspoon fresh rosemary, finely chopped
6 ounces blue cheese, crumbled Gorgonzola
1/2 cup sun-dried tomatoes, chopped
1/2 teaspoon fresh ground pepper

This all-in-one entree is nicely accompanied with any Great Lakes dry or semi-dry white wine.

Marinate chicken breasts and mushrooms in a prepared Caesar Salad dressing, overnight.

One hour before preparing recipe, grill the mushrooms and chicken over medium heat until pink just disappears in meat (do not over cook). Set aside in glass bowl and cover. Discard marinade.

Saute onions and garlic in olive oil in 6-8 quart pot while bringing chicken stock and wine to a boil in a separate sauce pan (add any juice from the standing grilled chicken). Mix rice into onion and garlic mixture, constantly stirring until all the rice grains are coated with oil. Stir in the boiling liquid mixture until throughly blended. Cover and turn heat to low. Simmer for exactly 20 minutes without removing the cover. While rice is simmering, prepare remaining ingredients and cut grilled chicken into cubes. Mix all ingredients into the chicken bowl (don't lose any of the juices).

As soon as 20 minutes has elapsed, take cover off rice and add the ingredient mixture. Blend throughly. Replace cover and allow to simmer for 3-5 minutes or until rice has a firm, but not hard feel to the teeth - "al dente".

Serve immediately in individual portions. Garnish with fresh parsley.

Per serving: 398 Calories; 13g Fat (31% calories from fat); 31g Protein; 35g Carbohydrate; 65mg Cholesterol; 727mg Sodium

RECIPES FROM THE WINERIES

Herbed Potatoes

From St. Julian Wine Co., Michigan

Serves 4

4 medium potatoes,
   sliced into 8 wedges
1/2 cup red wine vinegar
   w/ Italian seasonings
4 tablespoons oil
1 1/2 teaspoons rosemary
1 1/2 teaspoons parsley
1 teaspoon basil
1 teaspoon fresh ground pepper
1 teaspoon salt

A wonderful addition to any dinner. This dish goes especially well with lamb or roasted chicken and St. Julian Chancellor.

Wash potatoes with skin and place wedges in baking dish. In a small bowl combine the red wine vinegar and oil (St. Julian produces a special red wine seasoned vinegar dressing/marinade). Brush the potatoes with half of this mixture. Bake at 400 degrees F. for 25 minutes. Brush potatoes with remaining dressing mixture and bake for 15 more minutes. Sprinkle with remaining ingredients and bake for an additional 10 minutes.

Per serving: 192 Calories; 14g Fat (63% calories from fat); 2g Protein; 16g Carbohydrate; 0mg Cholesterol; 541mg Sodium

NOTES

_____

_____

_____

_____

_____

_____

_____

Linguine with Chardonnay Clam Sauce

From Ferrante Winery & Ristorante, Ohio

Serves 8

30 ounces clams, canned with liquid
1 cup Chardonnay
1/4 cup fresh parsley, chopped
1 teaspoon salt
1 tablespoon pepper
1 tablespoon garlic, crushed
1/2 cup flour
2 pounds linguine, cooked al dente

This popular seafood pasta dish is delicately complemented by a glass of Ferrante Select Chardonnay.

Drain clam juice into 2 quart saucepan and bring to boil.

Add parsley, salt, pepper and garlic. Cook for 1 minute. Add wine and continue on low boil for 2 more minutes. Slowly add flour to thicken. Add clams. When clams are heated, serve over al dente pasta.

Per serving: 476 Calories; 2g Fat (4% calories from fat); 16g Protein; 92g Carbohydrate; 3mg Cholesterol; 506mg Sodium

NOTES

_____

_____

_____

_____

_____

_____

_____

Morel Mushrooms in Wine Sauce

From L. Mawby Vineyards, Michigan

Serves 4

4 cups morels
1 tablespoon olive oil
1 medium onion, halved and slivered
3 cloves garlic, diced
14 ounces nonfat chicken broth
1/8 cup soy sauce
1/2 cup dry red wine
2 tablespoons balsamic vinegar
1/2 teaspoon thyme
1/4 teaspoon sage
1 teaspoon salt
2 tablespoons cornstarch

From the morel haven of Northern Michigan comes this flavorful pasta sauce accompanied by L. Mawby "Eric the Red" wine.

Wash morel mushrooms in cool water. Soak for 20 minutes in salted water. Drain. Rinse several times. Drain well on paper towels. Cut morels in half or into 2-inch pieces. Steam the morels over low heat in covered pan. Simmer for 20 minutes. Drain, reserving the juice.

Saute onion and garlic in olive oil until over medium heat stirring frequently to avoid burning until caramelized.

Mix together in bowl: chicken broth, soy, wine, balsamic vinegar, thyme, sage and salt. Add to onion/garlic mixture. Add reserved mushroom juice. Cover and return to simmer for 10 minutes.

Remove 1/2 cup liquid from pan. Return morels to pan.

Add constarch to the 1/2 cup liquid and wisk to a slurry.

Add slurry to pan and simmer until starch thickens and becomes clear (2-4 minutes).

Serve immediately over linguine pasta or rice.

Per serving: 105 Calories; 4g Fat (37% calories from fat); 3g Protein; 11g Carbohydrate; 0mg Cholesterol; 1209mg Sodium

Old World Spaghetti Sauce

From Joe Borrello

Serves 10

2 pounds pork loin, whole
2 tablespoons olive oil
6 ounces tomato paste
30 ounces tomatoes, canned,
   crushed in puree
1 cup red wine
2 cups water
2 leaves bay leaf
2 tablespoons basil leaves,
   fresh preferred
1 tablespoon oregano, dried or fresh
1 tablespoon fresh parsley
4 cloves garlic, finely chopped
1 large onion, finely chopped
4 ounces roasted red peppers,
   finely chopped
salt and pepper to taste

> Choose a hearty,
> dry red wine from the
> Great Lakes and any
> shape of pasta your
> heart desires.

Brown pork loin or roast (or substitute with Italian sausage links) in olive oil in 6-8 quart heavy pot. Take out meat, cover and set aside. Saute finely chopped onion and garlic in the meat fat and oil until translucent. Add rest of ingredients. Blend well and bring to hard boil over medium-high heat, then down to lowest heat to simmer for about 4 to 5 hours.

Put pork roast into sauce just after heat is turned down. If using Italian sausage or JOE'S ITALIAN MEATBALLS (see recipe) put in during the last two hours of simmering. Let stand overnight in refrigerator or cool place.

Skim excess surface fat next day and simmer another 2-3 hours. Add water or wine if too thick. Boil with cover off if too thin.

Makes enough sauce for up to two pounds of pasta. Freeze leftover sauce.

NOTE: The longer and slower the simmer - the better!

Per serving: 223 Calories; 12g Fat (52% calories from fat); 16g Protein; 10g Carbohydrate; 45mg Cholesterol; 243mg Sodium

Pasta Salad with Sun-Dried Tomato and Olive Pesto

From Lakeshore Winery, New York

Serves 8

1 pound pasta, cooked and cooled
3 ounces sun-dried tomatoes, dry-packed
boiling water
3 cloves garlic, whole but peeled
5 large fresh basil leaves, rinsed and drained
1/4 teaspoon salt
1/2 cup extra-virgin olive oil
1/4 cup Romano cheese, grated Pecorino
1/2 teaspoon dried oregano
3 ounces pitted black olives, drained
1/8 cup dry red wine

This pasta recipe can be served hot or cold and makes a delicious topping for toasted French or Italian bread. All would be for naught, however, without Lakeshore Country Clare, a dry red wine.

Place tomatoes in a jar or small bowl and pour in just enough boiling water to cover them. Allow to stand for at least 20 minutes, stirring occasionally to make sure all tomatoes are soaked. Put the tomatoes along with their soaking liquid into a blender or food processor, add the remaining ingredients and process about 30 seconds or longer depending on desired texture. Add desired amount of sauce (about 1/2 to 2/3 cup) to the pasta and stir to coat thoroughly. The remaining sauce can be kept refrigerated or frozen.

Per serving: 388 Calories; 17g Fat (39% calories from fat); 10g Protein; 50g Carbohydrate; 4mg Cholesterol; 428mg Sodium

NOTES

_____

_____

_____

_____

_____

Spinach Lasagna

From Leelanau Cellars, Michigan

Serves 8

1 pound lasagna noodles
16 ounces tomatoes, chopped
6 ounces tomato paste
1/2 cup dry red wine, Baco Noir
2 tablespoons olive oil
1 medium onion, chopped
4 cloves garlic, minced
1 teaspoon sugar
1/2 teaspoon oregano
1/2 teaspoon basil
1 teaspoon salt
2 packages frozen spinach, chopped and drained
1 large egg
16 ounces ricotta cheese or cottage cheese
1/4 cup Parmesan cheese
12 ounces mozzarella cheese, grated or sliced

"A Taste of Northern Michigan" with Leelanau Cellars Baco Noir.

Cook noodles according to package directions. Drain, rinse and set aside. Saute onions and garlic in oil until tender. Add chopped tomatoes, tomato paste and 1/2 cup of dry red wine.

Stir in sugar, salt, oregano and basil. Simmer for 15-20 minutes.

In a bowl put thawed, drained spinach, beaten egg, ricotta and parmesan cheese. Stir until mixed.

In a greased 9 by 13 pan put 1 layer of cooked noodles. Follow with 1/3 of tomato sauce, 1/2 of spinach mixture, 1/3 of mozzarella. Layer one more and end with noodles, sauce and mozzarella.

Bake at 350 degrees F. for 35-45 minutes uncovered.

Per serving: 558 Calories; 24g Fat (39% calories from fat); 28g Protein; 57g Carbohydrate; 91mg Cholesterol; 688mg Sodium

Three Star Goulash

From L. Mawby Vineyards, Michigan

Serves 8

2 pounds ground veal
4 tablespoons butter
1 cup dry red wine
4 stalks celery, diced
1/2 green pepper, diced
6 medium onions, chopped
12 cloves garlic, whole
2 tablespoons dried parsley
1 tablespoon dried basil
2 tablespoons herbal salt substitute
1 tablespoon onion powder
1 tablespoon fennel seed
2 quarts tomato juice
1 tablespoon dried parsley
1/2 tablespoon onion powder
1/2 tablespoon basil
3 tablespoons chili powder
1 tablespoon cumin powder
1 pound elbow macaroni

A hearty Great Lakes meal with whole wheat bread, salad and a bottle of L. Mawby Turkey Red or Foch.

Fry veal in butter. Add wine, celery, green pepper, onion and garlic. Add parsley, basil, salt, onion powder and fennel seed. Simmer until liquid is absorbed.

Add tomato juice, parsley, onion powder, basil, chili powder and cumin powder. Bring to bubbling simmer. Add pasta and simmer 20 minutes.

Per serving: 540 Calories; 15g Fat (26% calories from fat); 34g Protein; 64g Carbohydrate; 108mg Cholesterol; 1499mg Sodium

NOTES

Thunder and Lightning

From Michigan Vintner Wine Co., Michigan

Serves 4

8 ounces pasta, Orrecchietta cut
1/4 cup extra virgin olive oil
3 cloves garlic, peeled & minced
2 cups garbanzo beans, canned, drained
1 teaspoon dried sage
1 cup chicken stock
1/2 cup dry white wine
1 1/2 teaspoons cracked black pepper
2 tablespoons butter
1/2 cup grated parmesan cheese

These "pasta ears" present a delicious dish made and served with Michigan Vintner Seyval or Chardonel.

Cook pasta "al dente," drain and blend in butter.

In 10-12" skillet, heat oil, add garlic and garbanzos (chick peas) and cook over high heat until the garbanzos start to pop.

Add sage, stock, wine and pepper. Lower heat and cook until liquid is reduced by 1/2 and starts to thicken (at this point you may add spinach leaves, sorrel, escarole or arugula, if desired.)

Add a 1/4 cup of the grated cheese, garbanzos and broth mixture to the pasta. Toss well and serve immediately in warm bowls with Italian bread and remaining cheese.

Per serving: 604 Calories; 25g Fat (38% calories from fat); 19g Protein; 72g Carbohydrate; 23mg Cholesterol; 803mg Sodium

NOTES

_____

_____

_____

_____

_____

Vegetable Smothered Linguine

From L. Mawby Vineyards, Michigan

Serves 4

4 tablespoons butter
2 small onions, finely diced
1 cup dry white wine
2 tablespoons flour
1 cup milk
1/4 teaspoon herbal salt substitute
1/4 teaspoon white pepper
2 tablespoons Veg-It® prepared herb mix
1 tablespoon sugar
2 cups fresh carrots, julienned
1 1/2 cups green peas, fresh or frozen
2 cups cauliflower florets, fresh
1 1/2 cups broccoli florets, fresh
8 ounces linguine (spinach, carrot or whole wheat)
Parmesan cheese, freshly grated

> A vegetarian's delight along with a glass of L. Mawby Vignoles.

Steam vegetables, reserving 1 1/2 cups of water used in steamer. Saute onions in butter until transparent. Add wine and simmer to reduce by half. Blend flour a bit at a time until thickened. Remove from heat and allow to cool slightly. Add water from steamed vegetables slowly blending until smooth. Add milk. Heat briefly.

Add salt, pepper, Veg-It®, sugar, blend well, remove from heat. Add vegetables, correct seasoning to taste, simmer in double boiler until heated thoroughly.

Serve over cooked linguine with cheese sprinkled over top.

Per serving: 313 Calories; 14g Fat (44% calories from fat); 9g Protein; 31g Carbohydrate; 39mg Cholesterol; 468mg Sodium

NOTES

_____

_____

_____

White Bean Pasta Sauce

From Fox Run Vineyards, Finger Lakes, New York

Serves 4

1/3 cup extra virgin olive oil
4 cloves garlic, chopped
1/4 teaspoon red pepper flakes
2 stalks celery, finely chopped
19 ounces white kidney beans,
    drained and rinsed
1 large ripe tomato, cut in 1" cubes
1 teaspoon dried basil
1 teaspoon fresh parsley, chopped
salt to taste
fresh ground pepper (lots)

A peppery pasta sauce tamed
by Fox Run Chardonnay.

Heat oil, add celery and pepper flakes. Cook until celery softens. Add garlic and saute for 30 seconds. Add remaining ingredients, reduce heat, cook for 4-5 minutes.

Toss with hot pasta and serve with plenty of pepper and freshly grated Pecorino Romano or Parmesan cheese.

Per serving: 173 Calories; 18g Fat (92% calories from fat); 1g Protein; 3g Carbohydrate; 0mg Cholesterol; 19mg Sodium

NOTES

_____

_____

_____

_____

_____

_____

Wine & Wild Rice Bake

From von Stiehl Winery, Wisconsin

Serves 6

6 ounces wild rice, long-grained mix
1/2 cup onion, chopped
1/2 cup celery, chopped
2 tablespoons butter or margarine
1 can cream of mushroom soup, condensed, 10 3/4 oz. size
1/2 cup sour cream
1/3 cup dry white wine
1/2 teaspoon curry powder
2 cups chicken or turkey, cubed
1/4 cup fresh parsley

For a party buffet or a dinner entree, this dish will be a hit when served with von Stiehl Chenin Blanc wine.

Prepare rice mix according to directions indicated on package.

Saute onion, celery with butter in a saucepan until tender, but not brown. Blend in soup, sour cream, wine and curry powder. Stir in chicken or turkey and cooked rice.

Place mixture into a 12 x 7 x 2 baking pan and bake uncovered for 35-40 minutes at 350 degrees F. Stir before serving. Garnish with the parsley.

Per serving: 343 Calories; 16g Fat (43% calories from fat); 20g Protein; 28g Carbohydrate; 62mg Cholesterol; 563mg Sodium

NOTES

_____

_____

_____

_____

_____

_____

Winemaker's Spanish Rice

From Warner Vineyards, Michigan

Serves 4

1 pound hamburger
2 cups long-grain rice, uncooked
32 ounces tomatoes, coarsely chopped
1 medium onion, diced
1 medium green pepper, chopped
1 cup dry red wine
1 teaspoon chili powder
1/4 teaspoon fresh ground black pepper
salt to taste
2 cups water

A glass of Warner Cabernet Sauvignon or Chancellor should always be around when preparing and serving this dish.

Brown hamburger, onion and green pepper in a large pot. Add rice, tomatoes, spice, water and wine. Cover when mixture starts to boil. Cook on medium-low heat for 30 minutes or until rice is tender. Stir occasionally.

If needed, add a little more water while cooking.

Per serving: 691 Calories; 16g Fat (21% calories from fat); 18g Protein; 112g Carbohydrate; 44mg Cholesterol; 664mg Sodium

NOTES

_____

_____

_____

_____

_____

_____

_____

Poultry
& Fowl

Burgundy Chicken

From Arbor Hill Grapery, Finger Lakes, New York

Serves 2

2 skinless boneless chicken breast
  halves
2 tablespoons butter
1/4 cup onions, finely chopped
3 tablespoons red wine jelly
2 tablespoons red wine vinegar
1/4 cup heavy cream

Serve this dish with seasoned
or plain rice with Arbor Hill
wines and their delicious grape
condiment products.

In a heavy skillet melt butter and add chicken breasts. Cook 5 minutes, turn and cook 5 minutes more. Add onions and cook until chicken is tender. Remove chicken from skillet and place in warm oven.

Add jelly and wine vinegar to pan, scrape pan to deglaze. Boil one minute, stir in heavy cream, then stir and simmer until liquid is reduced and sauce is slightly thickened.

Place chicken on warm plates and cover with sauce. Serve immediately.

A catalog of Arbor Hill jellies, sauces, vinegars and preserves is available directly from the Grapery (see the winery listing).

Per serving: 309 Calories; 24g Fat (69% calories from fat); 21g Protein; 3g Carbohydrate; 122mg Cholesterol; 261mg Sodium

NOTES

_____

_____

_____

_____

_____

_____

Canadian Maple Chicken

From Kittling Ridge Estate Wines & Spirits, Ontario

Serves 4

4 boneless skinless chicken breast
   halves
2 teaspoons butter
1/4 cup Maple Brandy Liqueur
   * see note
1 teaspoon curry powder, mild

Kittling Ridge Maple Brandy
Liqueur gives this dish its special
flavor, but apple brandy or Calvados
may be used as a substitute.

Saute chicken until golden brown on both sides, reduce heat to low, cover
and cook for five minutes. Turn chicken and add Maple Liqueur, stir in curry,
cook covered for three minutes. Turn often.

For an added treat, use half-and-half and cook until thickened. Then
serve over rice or pasta.

*Maple Brandy Liqueur is available at Liquor Control Board of Ontario
(LCBO) retail stores or from the Kittling Ridge Retail Store (see winery
listings).

*Per serving: 119 Calories; 3g Fat (27% calories from fat); 21g Protein; 0g
Carbohydrate; 56mg Cholesterol; 79mg Sodium*

NOTES

_____

_____

_____

_____

_____

_____

_____

_____

Chicken in a Pot

From L. Mawby Vineyards, Michigan

Serves 6

2 each frying chickens quartered
1/2 cup olive oil
1 large onion, minced
1 clove garlic, minced
1 teaspoon salt
3/4 teaspoon pepper
1 medium tomato, diced
1/2 cup white wine, semi-dry

L. Mawby Sandpiper is the wine of choice for this Great Lakes country dish.

Brown chicken in olive oil. Sprinkle with onion, garlic, salt and pepper. Cover and simmer 30 minutes. Add tomato and wine. Simmer 30 minuites or until chicken is tender.

Per serving: 182 Calories; 18g Fat (94% calories from fat); 0g Protein; 2g Carbohydrate; 0mg Cholesterol; 450mg Sodium

NOTES

_____

_____

_____

_____

_____

_____

_____

_____

Chicken in Red Wine

From Fenn Valley Vineyards, Michigan

Serves 4

1/2 cup dry red wine
1/2 cup prunes, pitted and chopped
1/4 cup raisins
1/4 teaspoon ground cloves
1 1/2 pounds boneless skinless chicken
    breast halves
1/4 cup all-purpose flour
dash ground cinnamon
2 teaspoons olive oil
1 medium onion, finely chopped
1 clove garlic, thinly sliced
1/2 cup port wine
1/2 cup chicken broth, clear
1/4 teaspoon ground pepper
1/2 teaspoon vanilla extract

Serve this tasty dish over a bed of rice, noodles or couscous with a glass of Fenn Valley Lakeshore Red.

Combine chopped prunes, raisins and red wine in a small saucepan. Bring to a boil, remove from the heat, allow to cool to room temperature.

Rub the chicken breasts with the ground cloves. Mix the ground cinnamon into the flour. Dip the chicken in the flour to cover lightly. Saute the chicken in the olive oil over medium heat until lightly browned. Remove from the heat.

Reduce the heat to low and saute the onion and garlic until the onion is very soft. Add the port wine. Raise the heat to moderate and deglaze the pan. Add the prune mixture, the chicken broth, pepper and the chicken. Bring to a boil, lower the heat to low, cover and simmer until the chicken is cooked (15-20 minutes).

Remove the chicken to the serving platter. Bring the liquid to a boil and add the vanilla. If the sauce is thin, thicken with a mixture of flour and water. Pour over the chicken.

Per serving: 400 Calories; 6g Fat (15% calories from fat); 43g Protein; 31g Carbohydrate; 99mg Cholesterol; 454mg Sodium

Chicken Marsala

From Old Firehouse Winery, Ohio

Serves 8

8 chicken breast halves without skin, boned
flour
salt and pepper to taste
3 tablespoons olive oil
1 medium onion, sliced
2 cloves garlic, crushed
1/4 cup Chardonnay
1/2 cup sweet Marsala wine

Firehouse Cellars Chardonnay is the perfect wine for this tasty dish.

Pound the breasts into thin, consistent pieces. Coat the chicken in the flour after flavoring it with salt and pepper to taste.

Saute the onion and garlic in 1 tablespoon of olive oil until clear, not brown. Remove from the pan and deglaze the pan with the Chardonnay. Pour the liquid over the onion and garlic. Set this mixture aside.

Rinse the pan and heat again. Add 2 tablespoons of olive oil and saute the chicken pieces, a few at a time quickly on both sides, until they just begin to brown. Remove them to a warm plate as you cook all the pieces. Add the onion, garlic and wine mixture to the pan and deglaze with the Marsala wine. Allow the sauce to cook down a bit then pour over the chicken pieces.

Per serving: 177 Calories; 6g Fat (35% calories from fat); 26g Protein; 1g Carbohydrate; 65mg Cholesterol; 142mg Sodium

NOTES

_____

_____

_____

_____

_____

Chicken Spiedini with Prosciutto and Gorgonzola

From Joe Borrello

Serves 4

4 chicken breast halves without skin, boned
4 ounces prosciutto, thinly sliced
4 ounces sun-dried tomatoes
2/3 cup blue cheese, crumbled Gorgonzola
1/2 teaspoon ground sage
1/4 cup walnuts, finely chopped
2 tablespoons extra virgin olive oil
1 cup dry white wine
salt and pepper to taste

A delicious, full-flavored entree accompanied by a cheese and cream risotto or pasta. Don't forget a glass of Great Lakes Pinot Gris, Chardonnay or Merlot.

Soften the sun-dried tomatoes by soaking them in warm water for 1/2 to 1 hour.

Place each chicken breast between two pieces of plastic wrap. Using a food mallet, pound until about 1/4 inch thick. Remove the plastic wrap and place the flattened pieces on a clean work surface.

Top each chicken breast with 1-ounce of prosciutto, one sun-dried tomato (laid widthwise), 1/4 of the crumbled Gorgonzola (Italian blue cheese), 1/8 teaspoon of sage and a fourth of the chopped walnuts.

Roll up the chicken breasts with the toppings and wrap tightly in plastic wrap. Refrigerate the newly-created spiedini rolls for at least 1 hour.

When ready to prepare, remove the plastic wrap from the chicken spiedini and secure with toothpicks. Sprinkle with salt and pepper.

In a large skillet heat oil until hot. Add spiedini and brown on all sides. Turn frequently. Add wine and simmer covered for 10 to 15 minutes, depending on the thickness of the spiedini rolls.

Remove spiedini rolls to a clean cutting board and cover with foil to keep warm.

Reduce wine to half over medium-high heat. Strain into a glass bowl.

Slice each chicken spiedini vertically into 1/4 to 1/2 inch slices. Place slices, slightly overlapping each other, on individual dishes. Drizzle with wine sauce and serve.

Per serving: 430 Calories; 18g Fat (40% calories from fat); 42g Protein; 17g Carbohydrate; 99mg Cholesterol; 1697mg Sodium

Coq au Vin Longworth

From Chef Tom Johnson, Meier's Wine Cellars, Ohio

Serves 6

2 broiler chickens, cut up
8 ounces bacon, thick-sliced,
   cut in 1/4" pieces
8 ounces shiitake mushrooms, sliced
1 large shallot, minced
2 cloves garlic, peeled and minced
1/2 cup flour for dredging
salt to taste
fresh ground pepper
1/2 cup apricot brandy
12 boiling onions, cross cut, root end
1 bay leaf
2 sprigs parsley
3 sprigs thyme
2 cloves
2 tablespoons tomato paste
1 1/2 cups Catawba sweet wine
1 1/2 cups chicken stock or veal stock
3 tablespoons butter
1 tablespoon vegetable oil
2 tablespoons flour, sifted
3 tablespoons water
minced parsley for garnish

> Meier's American
> Catawba wine is the
> special twist to this
> classic French dish.

    Crisp the bacon pieces in an oven-proof casserole or Dutch oven, in a mixture of 1 tbls. butter and the oil. Remove the bacon pieces from the fat with a slotted spoon. Reserve bacon on a paper towel.

    Very lightly flour the chicken pieces, by shaking them in a paper bag containing a half cup of flour. Brown the chicken pieces in the mixture of bacon dripping, butter and oil. Then flame the chicken pieces with the brandy. Cover and sweat the chicken over low heat for about 10 minutes. Remove the chicken pieces to a plate and sprinkle with salt and pepper. Reserve.

    Add the boiling onions to the pan and brown them. Remove onions and reserve.

    Pour all of the browning grease out of the pan and replace with a single

tablespoon of fresh butter. Now lightly saute the shallot and garlic, taking care that they do not burn. Add the wine and stock to the pan, scraping any encrusted meat juices from the inside of the pan, into the sauce. Stir in the tomato paste and add the bouquet garni (the bay leaf, parsley, thyme and cloves tied in dampened cheesecloth).

Return the chicken pieces, the bacon and the onions to the sauce. Cover and simmer 30 minutes over medium-low heat or bake in a preheated 350 degree F. oven.

While the chicken is braising, lightly saute the mushrooms (portabellas made be used as a substitution) in a tablespoon of butter. Reserve. When the chicken has braised 25 minutes, add the mushrooms to the casserole and simmer an additional 5 minutes.

After the full 30 minutes of simmering, using a slotted spoon, remove the chicken pieces, mushrooms and onions to a warm platter. Lightly drape with foil and keep warm. Over high heat, reduce the sauce by 50%. Thicken with a slurry made of the 2 tablespoons of flour and the water, adding it gradually until the desired thickness is reached. Simmer an additional 5 minutes, then spoon over the platter of chicken. Sprinkle with minced fresh parsley. Serve at once.

Per serving: 642 Calories; 29g Fat (42% calories from fat); 25g Protein; 66g Carbohydrate; 47mg Cholesterol; 966mg Sodium

NOTES

_____

_____

_____

_____

_____

Country Chicken Piccata

From Bowers Harbor Vineyards, Michigan

Serves 4

2 pounds skinless boneless chicken breast halves
1/2 cup seasoned flour
3 tablespoons olive oil
1 pound fettucine
2 bunches broccoli, fresh
1 bottle Chardonnay
1/4 pound butter
1/4 cup lemon juice
capers
2 tablespoons fresh parsley, chopped

> Served with Bowers Harbor
> Vineyards Chardonnay Reserve.

Dredge chicken in seasoned flour. Saute in light olive oil until golden brown. Bake at 350 degrees F. for 15 minutes.

Cook fettucine as directed.

Trim and blanche broccoli in boiling, salted water.

Reduce wine by half in separate pan and remove from heat. Slowly add butter. Add capers and lemon juice.

Warm plates, put pasta in four equal servings on plates and place chicken on top.

Place broccoli around pasta. Pour sauce over pasta and garnish with chopped fresh parsley.

Per serving: 995 Calories; 39g Fat (36% calories from fat); 69g Protein; 89g Carbohydrate; 194mg Cholesterol; 410mg Sodium

NOTES

Duck Breast in a Black Currant Glaze

From Chef Eric Peacock, Henry of Pelham Winery, Ontario

Serves 4

1 1/2 pounds duck meat breasts
3 tablespoons black currants,
   dried or fresh
1/2 cup cassis liqueur
1/4 cup whipping cream

Classic and elegant with a glass of Henry of Pelham Cabernet/Merlot.

Pre-heat oven to 375 degrees F. and put oven-proof dry skillet (cast iron, if available) on a medium high stove burner.

Place duck breasts skin down in the dry pan to render the fat. As duck fat melts in the pan, remove breast and drain the fat into a disposable container. You may need to do this about 6 times to render the fat properly and give the crisp skin we are looking for.

Turn breasts flesh side down and cook in the oven for about 7-9 minutes.

When the duck has finished, remove pan from the oven and place breasts on a cutting surface. Discard any fat.

Place the pan over high heat and add the cassis, currants and cream. Reduce to glaze-like consistency, about 4 minutes. Slice the breast as thin as you can and toss all slices in glaze to coat.

Mixture may be used to top a luncheon salad or for a special treat, place over a DUCK LIVER PATE sitting on folded GREEN ONION CREPES (see recipes).

Per serving: 635 Calories; 54g Fat (80% calories from fat); 14g Protein; 15g Carbohydrate; 114mg Cholesterol; 83mg Sodium

NOTES

_____

_____

_____

_____

Fresh-Thyme Roasted Cornish Game Hens

From Chef Erik Peacock, Hernder Estate Winery, Ontario

Serves 4

4 Cornish game hens
1 onion, quartered
2 teaspoons fresh thyme, minced
4 cloves garlic, peeled
8 teaspoons dry red wine
salt and pepper

FOR SAUCE

4 shallots, finely diced
2 tablespoons olive oil
2 tablespoons Dijon mustard
1 cup chicken stock
1/2 cup dry red wine
4 tablespoons butter, ice cold
salt and pepper

A flavorful dish served with wild rice and a bottle of Hernder Estate Merlot.

Preheat oven to 375 degrees F.

Sprinkle salt, pepper and thyme in cavity of each hen. Place 2 teaspoons of wine in each cavity with onion and garlic. Place hens in the oven for approximately 50 minutes.

Heat oil in saucepan and gently cook shallots for about 3-4 minutes. Add wine, stock and mustard. Wisk until incorporated. Turn heat to high and reduce by half. Reserve until hens are almost finished. Birds are done when the juices run clear.

Bring sauce up to a boil and wisk in cold butter to thicken the sauce. Serve immediately.

Per serving: 1578 Calories; 96g Fat (57% calories from fat); 157g Protein; 8g Carbohydrate; 527mg Cholesterol; 2319mg Sodium

Grilled Chicken Moutard

From Hunt Country Vineyards, Finger Lakes, New York

Serves 4

4 skinless boneless chicken breast
  halves, chargrilled
2 cups heavy cream
3 tablespoons shallots, chopped
1/2 cup Dijon mustard
salt and pepper to taste
3 tablespoons parsley, chopped
1 teaspoon lemon juice
2 tablespoons butter
2 tablespoons flour

Excellent when accompanied by a light pasta or rice side dish and grilled vegetables. Hunt Country Chardonnay would be the perfect wine.

   Melt butter in saucepan, add flour, cook until thick paste (about 2 minutes).
   Add remaining ingredients and simmer until sauce is creamy. Place on warm plate with chicken.

Per serving: 610 Calories; 53g Fat (76% calories from fat); 26g Protein; 11g Carbohydrate; 230mg Cholesterol; 552mg Sodium

NOTES

_____

_____

_____

_____

_____

_____

_____

_____

Pollo Vino Al Lamponi (Chicken Raspberry)

From Ferrante Winery & Ristorante, Ohio

Serves 8

8 skinless boneless chicken breast halves
6 cups fresh raspberries
2 cups semi-dry white wine
2 cups corn syrup, white
4 ounces cornstarch
2 tablespoons olive oil
8 fresh mint leaves

Pair this impressive chicken dish with a glass of fruity Ferrante White Catawba.

Boil fresh raspberries in 2 quart saucepan.

Drain and add wine. Bring to boil and add syrup. Cook 2 minutes. Add cornstarch to thicken.

In separate pan using hot olive oil, saute chicken until done. Serve chicken over raspberry sauce and garnish with fresh mint leaf.

Per serving: 459 Calories; 5g Fat (10% calories from fat); 21g Protein; 86g Carbohydrate; 51mg Cholesterol; 161mg Sodium

NOTES

_____

_____

_____

_____

_____

_____

_____

Poule au Pot (Chicken in a Pot)

From Chef Tom Johnson, Firelands Winery, Ohio

Serves 4

4 medium carrots, peeled and halved
2 large leeks
4 stalks celery
1 turnip, finely diced
3 sprigs fresh tarragon
6 stems parsley
1 large bay leaf
3 whole cloves
4 chicken breast halves
4 chicken drumsticks
4 chicken thighs
4 tablespoons unsalted butter
2 tablespoons canola oil
1 1/2 cups semi-dry white wine
1 1/2 cups chicken broth
sea salt & fresh ground black pepper

Here is the classic French country dish made famous by King Henri IV, who vowed that a chicken would gently simmer in wine and broth, in every Frenchman's cook pot. Try Firelands Winery Vidal Blanc or Gewurztraminer and crusty bread with this one.

Halve the carrots, leeks and celery lengthwise. Bias-cut these vegetables in 3-inch pieces. Combine with the diced turnip and reserve.

Prepare a "bouquet garni" by combining the green tops of the leeks, leaves from the celery stalks, tarragon, parsley, bay leaf and whole cloves tied in a dampened cheesecloth. Reserve.

In a large casserole, heat 2 tablespoons of butter over moderate heat. Lightly saute the vegetables for 5 minutes, then remove them to a bowl and reserve them while browning the chicken.

Add the remaining butter and the canola oil to the skillet and over moderate heat, lightly brown the chicken pieces. This will require about 10 minutes. Then, tip the cooking vessel and pour out any remaining fat. Return the vegetables to the chicken in the pot, bury the "bouquet garni" in the vegetables, add the wine and the chicken broth. Bring to simmer, covering and very gently simmering for 15 minutes. Lift out the breast pieces and reserve them on a warm platter, draped with foil. Braise the dark meat about 5 minutes longer, then remove to the platter with the breast pieces. Spoon the vegetables over the chicken and sprinkle them with salt and pepper. Serve in deep, rimmed soup plates, passing the broth on the side.

Per serving: 1089 Calories; 60g Fat (47% calories from fat); 87g Protein; 64g Carbohydrate; 266mg Cholesterol; 1308mg Sodium

Poulet D'Andree

From Chateau des Charmes, Ontario

Serves 4

1/4 cup flour
salt to taste
freshly ground pepper
1 roasting chicken, cut into parts
1 tablespoon cooking oil
1/4 cup butter
1/4 cup chopped onion or shallot
1 1/2 cups button mushrooms, sliced
1 1/2 cups dry white wine
1 1/4 cups chicken stock
3 medium tomatoes, chopped
1 sprig fresh tarragon, chopped
1 sprig fresh chervil, chopped
1 sprig fresh parsley, chopped

Chateau des Charmes
V.Q.A. Riesling or
Chardonnay would
make a perfect dinner
companion for this
hearty dish.

Season the flour with salt and pepper, and use to dust the chicken portions. Heat the oil and butter in a frying pan, and fry the chicken pieces until tender and browned all over, allowing 15-20 minutes for dark meat and 10-12 minutes for light meat.

When tender, remove from the pan, drain on soft paper towels, and transfer to a warmed serving dish. Cover loosely and keep hot.

Put the onion or shallot into the pan with the fat in which the chicken was cooked, fry gently without coloring. Add the mushrooms to the pan and continue frying until tender. Pour in the wine, add the chopped tomatoes and the stock. Stir until well blended, then simmer gently for 10 minutes.

Add most of the herbs to the sauce, and season to taste. Pour the sauce over the chicken, sprinkle with the remaining herbs and serve very hot.

Per serving: 986 Calories; 69g Fat (67% calories from fat); 62g Protein; 14g Carbohydrate; 275mg Cholesterol; 714mg Sodium

Puffed Polo

From St. Julian Wine Company, Michigan

Serves 4

1 teaspoon garlic, minced
2 carrots, peeled and chopped
1/2 cup butter
1/2 green bell pepper, sliced thin
2 skinless boneless chicken breast halves
1 cup flour
2 tablespoons butter
1 pound mushrooms thinly sliced
1 cup dry white wine
1 teaspoon parsley
1/2 teaspoon basil
 salt and pepper to taste
1 sheet frozen puff pastry
1 egg
1 tablespoon water

A splendid dish with the extra added touch of St. Julian Great White wine.

   In a skillet, saute the garlic, carrots and bell pepper in 1/2 cup of butter. Cook until the carrots are soft. Remove vegetables and add the 2 tablespoons of butter to the same skillet. Flour the chicken breasts and saute until each side is glazed. Add the mushrooms, wine, parsley, basil, salt and pepper. Simmer for 3 minutes. Divide puff pastry into 4 squares. Place chicken breast on pastry. Top with vegetable mixture and mushrooms. Fold dough over vegetables, leaving no holes. Beat egg, water and brush this mixture over the dough. Bake in 375 degree F. oven for 30 minutes or until browned.

Per serving: 516 Calories; 31g Fat (57% calories from fat); 18g Protein; 34g Carbohydrate; 147mg Cholesterol; 354mg Sodium

NOTES

_____

_____

_____

Raspberry Chicken a la Orange

From Heritage Wine Cellars, Pennsylvania

Serves 6

6 boned and skinned chicken breast halves
1/2 cup raspberry wine
1/2 cup orange juice
1 tablespoon olive oil
1 teaspoon rosemary
1 teaspoon white pepper
1 teaspoon garlic powder
1 medium onion, sliced
1 cup shiitake mushrooms, sliced

Delicious with rice pilaf, steamed string beans with almonds and Heritage Raspberry wine, of course!

Spray casserole or roasting pan with Pam. Arrange chicken breasts in the cooking container (not aluminum). Mix wine, orange juice and olive oil, pour over chicken and marinate in refrigerator for one hour.

Blend herbs, sprinkle over chicken. Arrange onion slices and mushrooms on top of chicken.

Bake covered for one hour at 350 degrees F.

Per serving: 173 Calories; 4g Fat (20% calories from fat); 22g Protein; 13g Carbohydrate; 51mg Cholesterol; 153mg Sodium

NOTES

_____

_____

_____

_____

_____

_____

_____

Roman Chicken Bastilla

From Chef Carla Reid, Kittling Ridge Estate, Ontario

Serves 6

A unique second course when served with Kittling Ridge Chardonnay.

BOTTOM LAYER
2 cups ricotta cheese, part skim milk
1/2 cup Parmesan cheese, grated
1 cup mozzarella cheese, grated
1 egg beaten
salt
1 pinch ground nutmeg
9 sheets phyllo pastry
1/3 cup butter melted

TOP LAYER
2 tablespoons olive oil
1/4 cup onion, chopped
1/3 cup green bell pepper, chopped
1/3 cup sweet red pepper, chopped
1 medium zucchini, sliced
1 cup fresh mushrooms, sliced
1/2 teaspoon minced garlic
2 boneless skinless chicken breast
  halves, diced
1 tablespoon sun-dried tomatoes,
  chopped
1 1/2 teaspoons fresh basil, minced
2 tablespoons fresh parsley,
chopped
1/4 cup Chardonnay
1 1/2 cups tomato sauce
salt and pepper

BOTTOM LAYER

Brush first sheet of phyllo pastry with melted butter, totally covering the entire area. Place in 10 inch springform pan leaving the edges over the sides. Butter 5 more phyllo pastry sheets placing them in the springform so that they evenly cover the pan.

Mix cheese, egg and spices together. Spread evenly in the pan over the pastry.

TOP LAYER

Heat oil in a pan. Add the onion and saute for 1 minute. Add peppers, zucchini and mushrooms. Saute for another minute. Stir in garlic and chicken and saute until the chicken turns white. Add sun-dried tomatoes, basil, parsley and Chardonnay. Saute for another minute then pour in the tomato sauce. Season with salt and pepper. Simmer slowly for 8-10 minutes.

Place over cheese mixture and fold over the ends of phyllo pastry to cover the top. Brush the remaining pastry sheets with butter and bunch on the top to form a flower effect. Bake at 350 degrees F. until pastry is golden brown about 35 to 40 minutes. Cool slightly then release from springform pan.

Per serving: 500 Calories; 31g Fat (56% calories from fat); 28g Protein; 27g Carbohydrate; 122mg Cholesterol; 959mg Sodium

Spicy Svenska Chicken

From Swedish Hill Vineyard, Finger Lakes, New York

Serves 6

2 teaspoons salt or to taste
3 each scallions, chopped
1/4 teaspoon allspice, optional
1/2 teaspoon cinnamon
1/2 cup dry white wine
1 cup heavy cream
6 each boned and skinned chicken
   breast, halves
1/2 cup black olives, halved
1/4 cup butter
1/4 cup parsley, chopped

A taste of the Old Country with this chicken dish and a glass of Swedish Hill Cayuga White.

Preheat oven to 300 degrees F., preheat baking dish. Mix salt, allspice and cinnamon and sprinkle on both sides of meat. Melt butter in heavy skillet. Saute breasts one minute over low heat. Turn and saute one more minute. Transfer to hot baking dish. Place in oven and bake 10 minutes. While breasts are cooking, add scallions to remaining butter, raise heat. When scallions are soft, stir in wine and cream. Cook over high heat to reduce liquid (be careful not to "break" the cream). Stir in pan juices from breasts. Continue cooking until reduced by 1/2. Arrange chicken on platter and pour sauce over. Sprinkle with parsley and serve with wild rice.

Per serving: 341 Calories; 25g Fat (68% calories from fat); 22g Protein; 4g Carbohydrate; 126mg Cholesterol; 975mg Sodium

NOTES

_____

_____

_____

_____

_____

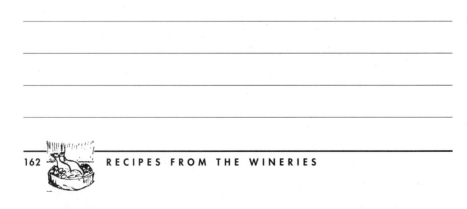

Strawberry Chicken

From Lake Michigan Winery, Indiana

Serves 4

4 each skinless boneless chicken breast
   halves, 8 oz. size
4 ounces fresh mushrooms, sliced
1/2 red bell pepper, diced
1/8 teaspoon white pepper
1/2 teaspoon basil dry, crushed
1/2 teaspoon rosemary dry, crushed
8 ounces strawberry wine
2 ounces butter
2 ounces olive oil

A flavorful chicken item using Lake Michigan Winery Strawberry wine and served with its Vignoles dinner wine.

Combine white pepper, basil and rosemary and rub onto the chicken breasts. Refrigerate for 30-60 minutes.

Combine olive oil and butter in a heavy skillet or saute pan over medium high heat. Add chicken breasts (do not crowd) and saute for 2-3 minutes on each side or until done to your liking. Remove to warm oven. Add the mushrooms and peppers and saute until tender, do not overcook.

Remove to platter with chicken breasts. Drain pan, but do not scrape.

Return to heat and add the wine. Scrape to loosen bits in pan (deglaze). Cook until reduced in volume by half. Pour over chicken, mushrooms and peppers.

Serve on a bed of white rice with steamed broccoli.

Per serving: 338 Calories; 27g Fat (72% calories from fat); 21g Protein; 2g Carbohydrate; 82mg Cholesterol; 178mg Sodium

NOTES

_____

_____

_____

_____

 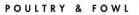

Tarragon Wine Stuffing

From McGregor Vineyard, Finger Lakes, New York

Serves 16

1 cup shallots, finely chopped
2 tablespoons tarragon
8 cups soft bread crumbs, mixed grain
1 cup sliced almonds, toasted
1/2 cup fresh parsley, chopped
3/4 cup melted butter
3/4 cup white wine, semi-dry
poultry seasoning, optional
chopped celery, optional

A Great Lakes stuffing for chicken or turkey and the setting for McGregor Cayuga White or Gewurztraminer.

Saute shallots in 6 tablespoons of the butter. Mix all ingredients until slightly moist. Refrigerate until ready to use.

Per serving: 552 Calories; 20g Fat (33% calories from fat); 14g Protein; 77g Carbohydrate; 23mg Cholesterol; 798mg Sodium

NOTES

_____

_____

_____

_____

_____

_____

_____

_____

Traverse Bay Chicken

From Leelanau Cellars, Michigan

Serves 4

2 1/2 pounds chicken, cut up
1/4 cup olive oil
2 medium onions, diced
2 cloves garlic, minced
1 pound tomatoes, chopped
8 ounces tomato sauce
1 teaspoon salt
1/4 teaspoon pepper
1 teaspoon oregano or basil
2 whole bay leaves
1/2 cup dry white wine

"A Taste of Northern Michigan" served with Leelanau Cellars Renaissance, Spring Splendor or Winter White.

Brown chicken in olive oil; remove from skillet. Add onions and garlic to drippings and saute until tender.

Add remaining ingredients, except wine. Return chicken to skillet and simmer 45 minutes covered.

Stir in the dry white wine. Uncover and turn occasionally and cook 20 minutes more or until tender.

Per serving: 558 Calories; 29g Fat (49% calories from fat); 53g Protein; 16g Carbohydrate; 155mg Cholesterol; 1312mg Sodium

NOTES

_____

_____

_____

_____

_____

_____

Turkey Breast in Vidal Cream Sauce

From Reif Estate Winery, Ontario

Serves 4

2 tablespoons extra virgin olive oil
2 small onions, cut into rings
8 turkey breast slices or scallops
2 tablespoons flour
1 3/4 cups semi-dry white wine, preferably Vidal
salt and pepper to taste
3 large red peppers, cut into rings
3/4 cup heavy cream

> Reif Estate Vidal wine is the secret ingredient that gives this delicate recipe a special taste.

Heat oil in skillet. Add onion and saute until soft. Coat turkey with flour seasoned with salt and pepper. Cook until brown on both sides. Remove from pan. Stir in the remaining flour. Gradually add the wine and bring to a boil. Return turkey to skillet, add red pepper rings. Reduce heat and simmer 15-20 minutes. Remove from heat and stir in cream. Simmer until thick. Serve over a bed of rice or fettuccine pasta.

Per serving: 303 Calories; 24g Fat (71% calories from fat); 12g Protein; 11g Carbohydrate; 78mg Cholesterol; 894mg Sodium

NOTES

_____

_____

_____

_____

_____

_____

Turkey Tetrazzini

From Hunt Country Vineyards, Finger Lakes, New York

Serves 4

3 cups cooked turkey, chopped
3 tablespoons butter
2 tablespoons flour
2 cups dry white wine
1/2 pound mushrooms, sauteed
1 cup whipping cream
1/2 pound spaghetti

This dish is aptly complemented by Hunt Country Foxy Lady white wine.

Make a sauce of the butter, flour and wine. Remove from heat and stir in whipping cream (room temp).

Cook spaghetti and preheat oven to 375 degrees F.

Add 1/2 the sauce to the turkey and 1/2 to the spaghetti and mushrooms.

Place spaghetti mixture in a greased casserole. Make a hole in the center and place the turkey mixture in it. Sprinkle with grated parmesan or romano cheese.

Bake until lightly browned and bubbly.

Per serving: 722 Calories; 35g Fat (49% calories from fat); 31g Protein; 51g Carbohydrate; 160mg Cholesterol; 172mg Sodium

NOTES

_____

_____

_____

_____

_____

_____

_____

Vintner's Chicken

From Warner Vineyards, Michigan

Serves 3

1 whole frying chicken, cut up
2/3 cup mushrooms, sliced
3/4 cup semi-dry white wine
1/2 teaspoon brown sugar
1/4 teaspoon poultry seasoning
salt and pepper to taste

Warner Vineyards suggests
their Chardonnay, Riesling
or Classic White with this
recipe. Take your pick.

Sprinkle pieces of chicken with poultry seasoning, salt and pepper.
Place skin-side down in shallow baking dish. Cover with mushrooms.
Dissolve sugar in wine, add to dish.
Place in 350 degree F. oven for 25 minutes. Turn chicken and finish
cooking until done, about 20 minutes.

*Per serving: 581 Calories; 24g Fat (39% calories from fat); 81g Protein; 6g
Carbohydrate; 247mg Cholesterol; 240mg Sodium*

NOTES

_____

_____

_____

_____

_____

_____

_____

Soups
& Salads

Autumn Celebration Bean Soup

From L. Mawby Vineyards, Michigan

Serves 12

2 1/2 cups dry white wine
2 medium onions, chopped
1 large carrot, grated
1 tablespoon parsley
1/4 teaspoon garlic powder
1 teaspoon celery seed
1 teaspoon dried basil
1 tablespoon Veg-It (commercial seasoning mix)*
1 tablespoon Vegetable Magic (commercial seasoning mix)
1 teaspoon salt
1 teaspoon dried mushroom powder
14 ounces nonfat chicken broth
3 sun-dried tomatoes in olive oil
1 cup frozen peas
1 cup frozen corn
1 cup carrots, diced
2 medium potatoes, diced
48 ounces Great Northern beans
8 tablespoons molasses
1 1/2 cups brown rice, instant

A hearty and healthy, stick-to-your-ribs soup featuring Leelanau Peninsula Pinot Gris from L. Mawby.

In a large kettle (preferably iron) mix the wine, onions, grated carrots, parsley, garlic powder, celery seed, dried basil, salt, seasoning mixes and mushroom powder. Simmer for 1 hour.

Add to the pot the chicken broth and dried tomatoes. Simmer for 1 hour. Pour pot contents into blender and puree.

Pour puree blend back into the kettle and add the peas, corn, diced carrots, potatoes and beans. Reheat to near boil and simmer 2 hours.

Add molasses and simmer 1 hour.

Add brown rice and simmer 1 hour.

*Veg-it and Vegetable Magic are prepared seasoning mixes found in the specialty food section of grocery or gourmet food stores.

Per serving: 622 Calories; 3g Fat (4% calories from fat); 31g Protein; 116g Carbohydrate; 0mg Cholesterol; 637mg Sodium

Black Bean Soup

From Fox Run Vineyards, Finger Lakes, New York

Serves 6

1 cup dried black beans, rinsed and
  drained
1 tablespoon extra virgin olive oil
1 large yellow onion, chopped
3 cloves garlic, minced
1 quart vegetable broth
4 carrots, sliced
4 medium tomatoes, red ripe, peel,
  seed & chop
1 green bell pepper, seeded and diced
1 red bell pepper, seeded and diced
2 tablespoons fresh parsley, chopped
1 tablespoon fresh thyme, chopped
1 tablespoon red wine vinegar
1/2 teaspoon mustard powder
1/4 teaspoon crushed red pepper
salt and pepper to taste

> This colorful soup is perfect with a glass of Fox Run Merlot.

Combine the beans with 3 cups of water and soak for 6 to 8 hours or overnight. Alternately, bring the water to a boil, add the beans and boil for 2 minutes. Remove from the heat, cover and let stand for one hour.

Heat the oil in a saucepan over medium heat. Add the onion and garlic and cook, stirring occasionally until the onion is tender, 5-7 minutes.

Drain the soaked beans and add to the pot along with the stock. Bring to a boil. Reduce the heat to a simmer, cover and cook for 1 hour.

Stir in the carrots, tomatoes, bell peppers, parsley, thyme, vinegar, powdered mustard and pepper flakes. Cover and simmer for an additional hour.

Per serving: 290 Calories; 6g Fat (17% calories from fat); 13g Protein; 49g Carbohydrate; 2mg Cholesterol; 1127mg Sodium

NOTES

_____

_____

Chicken Broth

From Michigan Vintner Wine Co., Michigan

Serves 8

Reserved bones from 2-3 chickens, raw or cooked
25 ounces Riesling wine, 1 bottle
2 1/2 quarts water
1 large onion, quartered
2 carrots, quartered
3 stalks celery with leaves
1 bunch fresh parsley
3 cloves garlic, peeled
2 bay leaves
15 whole black peppercorns
1 teaspoon seasoned salt

> Good broth is essential for all soups and sauces. It's even better when made with Michigan Vintner Riesling.

Brown bones in a large pressure cooker. Add wine plus 2 1/2 quarts of water and all remaining ingredients. Cook under pressure for an hour (or 3 hours in a stock pot.) Allow to cool slightly, strain and skim fat from broth. Be sure to save the fat - it is great for frying.

Broth can be frozen in plastic containers or freezer bags for up to six months.

Per serving: 111 Calories; 1g Fat (8% calories from fat); 2g Protein; 13g Carbohydrate; 0mg Cholesterol; 278mg Sodium

NOTES

_____

_____

_____

_____

_____

_____

Crayfish Soup

From Tabor Hill Winery, Michigan

Serves 6

4 cups water
1/2 teaspoon salt
1/4 teaspoon black pepper
1 medium onion, diced
1 carrot, diced
bouquet garni mix* see note
50 crayfish or 2 lbs. of shrimp
8 slices stale bread, crumbled
8 cups fish stock
1/4 cup dry white wine
3 tablespoons butter

A winery favorite and best when served with a bottle of Tabor Hill Gewurztraminer or Riesling wine.

Add diced carrot and onion to the water with salt, pepper and bouquet garni. Bring to a full rolling boil and put in the shellfish. Reduce heat and cook gently 15 minutes. Strain off liquid, but do not throw it away.

When the shellfish is cool enough to handle, extract the meat from the tails. Force the shells through a meat chopper or food processor, using the fine blade. Pound to a paste. Add the paste to 2 cups of the broth and simmer 5 minutes. Strain and return to the fire. Add the stock and bread crumbs. Stir until the bread has blended with the stock. Add the wine and the rest of the broth and bring to the boiling point, stirring constantly with a wooden spoon. Just before serving, add the meat and the butter. This soup must be served immediately.

*Bouquet garni is a mixture of herbs and seasonings, usually including parsley, celery, carrot or whatever else strikes the cook's fancy, tied in cheese-cloth and used to flavor sauces and soups. Remove before serving.

Per serving: 313 Calories; 15g Fat (52% calories from fat); 8g Protein; 23g Carbohydrate; 69mg Cholesterol; 847mg Sodium

NOTES

Cream of Brie Soup

From Northland Vineyards/Winery, Ohio

Serves 6

1/2 cup yellow onion, peeled
  and chopped
1/2 cup celery, thinly sliced
4 tablespoons butter
1/4 cup flour
2 cups milk
2 cups chicken broth
3/4 pound Brie, cubed
salt and pepper to taste
chives for garnish, chopped

A wonderful soup course for
a dinner party made even more
special when served with
Northland Vineyards
Chardonnay.

In a 3-quart saucepan, saute the onion and celery in the butter until limp. Stir in flour. Remove from heat. Stir in milk and chicken broth using a wisk to mix well. Return to heat and simmer, stirring constantly, until soup thickens. Add the Brie cheese (do not remove the rind). Stir until melted.

Run soup through a food processor or blender until very smooth. Correct seasoning with salt and pepper. Serve very hot with chive garnish.

Per serving: 357 Calories; 27g Fat (68% calories from fat); 19g Protein; 10g Carbohydrate; 89mg Cholesterol; 1004mg Sodium

NOTES

_____

_____

_____

_____

_____

_____

_____

Great White Garlic Soup

From St. Julian Wine Company, Michigan

Serves 8

1/3 cup unsalted butter
2 small onions, chopped
1/2 cup garlic, chopped
5 scallions, chopped
1/2 cup flour
5 cups beef broth
1 1/2 cups dry white wine
1/2 cup sour cream
1/2 teaspoon nutmeg
croutons

A creamy rich soup that goes great with crisp breadsticks and St. Julian Great White wine.

In a saucepan melt butter and saute the onion, garlic and scallions until soft. Stir in flour and cook for three minutes stirring constantly. Add the broth and wine. Bring to boil, then reduce to simmer for 20 minutes. Remove and cool to luke-warm. Puree and return to pan. Stir in the sour cream and nutmeg and reheat but do not boil. Serve with croutons.

Per serving: 233 Calories; 13g Fat (57% calories from fat); 9g Protein; 13g Carbohydrate; 30mg Cholesterol; 1130mg Sodium

NOTES

_____

_____

_____

_____

_____

_____

_____

Grilled Garlic Shrimp Salad

From Chef Erik Peacock, Hernder Estate Winery, Ontario

Serves 6

12 jumbo shrimp, peeled and deveined
3 cloves garlic, minced
2 tablespoons vegetable oil
2 tablespoons soy sauce
8 ounces arugula leaves
1 cup orange juice, freshly squeezed
1 teaspoon ginger minced
3 tablespoons brown sugar
1/4 teaspoon sesame oil
1/4 cup olive oil
1 cup adzuki beans, dried
4 tablespoons sesame seeds
3 pre-made crepes

On a hot summer day, this sophisticated salad and Hernder Estate Winery's Riesling/Traminer wine may be the only solution to beating the heat.

Soak dried beans for 24 hours. After soaking, simmer beans in approximately 8 cups of water for about 1 1/2 hours or until tender. Run cold water over beans until completely cool. Reserve beans until end.

Make a vinaigrette by whisking 1 tablespoon of soy sauce, orange juice, minced ginger, brown sugar and sesame oil with the olive oil. Reserve.

Cut crepes in triangles and fry in vegetable oil until firm. Drain on paper towel. Season with a dash of salt. Keep these uncovered until ready to use and garnish on the side or top of the salad.

1 hour before eating, toss the shrimp with 1 tablespoon of soy sauce, garlic and just enough vegetable oil to coat them.

In a 350 degrees F. oven, toast the sesame seeds in a frying pan for about 4-5 minutes. Reserve in a small dish.

Divide greens among six plates and sprinkle with beans and sesame seeds. Grill the garlic shrimp over hot coals.

Place cooked shrimp on the prepared plates and drizzle with vinaigrette.

Per serving: 370 Calories; 19g Fat (44% calories from fat); 20g Protein; 33g Carbohydrate; 77mg Cholesterol; 368mg Sodium

Lentil-Leek Soup with Fresh Ginger and Sherry

From Chef Tom Johnson, Meier's Wine Cellars, Ohio

Serves 8

1/2 pound lentils, dry
8 cups chicken stock
1/4 cup peanut oil
1/4 teaspoon Tabasco sauce
  or hot chili paste
2 cups leeks washed and chopped
1 tablespoon garlic, minced
1 teaspoon soy sauce
1/2 cup sherry medium-dry

A chef's favorite old recipe with some new twists, including Meier's #22 Sherry.

Place lentils in a large bowl. In a heavy saucepan, bring 6 cups of stock to boil and pour over the lentils. Let the lentils soak 15 minutes.

Meanwhile, in a heavy saucepan over medium-high heat, heat the oil. Add the Tabasco (try Sambal Olek, an Indonesian hot chili paste, if you can find it) and stir for a few seconds. Add the leeks (white parts with about only 2 inches of the green) and lightly saute 3 or 4 minutes, to soften. Add the ginger and garlic and saute, stirring another 2 minutes. Add the lentils and stock from the bowl, plus the remaining 2 cups of stock. Simmer until lentils are just tender, but not mushy, about 25 minutes. Remove from heat and add soy sauce and the sherry. Adjust seasonings to taste.

Per serving: 221 Calories; 8g Fat (37% calories from fat); 13g Protein; 20g Carbohydrate; 0mg Cholesterol; 817mg Sodium

NOTES

_____

_____

_____

_____

_____

Mama Mia's Chili

From Cedar Springs Wines, Ontario

Serves 8

1/2 pound ground beef
6 small green tomatoes,
  coarsely chopped
1 large onion, chopped
1 medium green pepper, chopped
1/2 cup mushrooms, chopped
2 cloves garlic, minced
2 tablespoons olive oil
15 ounces tomato sauce
15 ounces stewed tomatoes
16 ounces kidney beans, canned,
  drained
10 ounces bean and bacon soup,
  condensed
2 tablespoons chili sauce
2 tablespoons ketchup
1/2 cup dry red wine
3 beef frankfurters, cooked and
  sliced
1 teaspoon cumin
chili powder to taste
salt and pepper to taste
seasoned salt to taste

A bowl of homemade chili, garlic bread, a fresh garden salad and a glass of Cedar Springs Baco Noir - it doesn't get much better.

Brown beef; drain off fat and set aside. In a large pan, saute green tomatoes, onion, green pepper, mushrooms and garlic in oil. Add remaining ingredients and simmer 1 1/2 to 2 hours.

Can be made ahead and frozen.

Per serving: 314 Calories; 17g Fat (49% calories from fat); 13g Protein; 27g Carbohydrate; 35mg Cholesterol; 1105mg Sodium

Minted Pea Soup

From Fenn Valley Vineyards, Michigan

Serves 4

18 ounces frozen peas
2 cups chicken stock
1 cup white wine, semi-dry
2 large green onions, chopped
$1/2$ cup half and half
$1/2$ teaspoon mint, freshly chopped
salt and pepper to taste

A chilled soup with a cool bottle of Fenn Valley Lakeshore White.

Simmer peas, onions, stock and wine until peas are tender, about 6 minutes. Cool and puree. Season to taste with salt and fresh ground pepper.

Chill thoroughly. Before serving, stir in chopped mint and half & half.

Serve in glass bowls or wide-mouth wine glasses. Garnish with fresh mint sprigs.

Per serving: 221 Calories; 5g Fat (23% calories from fat); 11g Protein; 25g Carbohydrate; 11mg Cholesterol; 558mg Sodium

NOTES

_____

_____

_____

_____

_____

_____

_____

Mrs. C's Chicken Chardonnay Soup

From Casa Larga Vineyards, Finger Lakes, New York

Serves 10

1 tablespoon salt
1/3 cup apple cider vinegar
4 chicken breasts or a whole
   stewing chicken cut up
4 stalks celery
4 carrots, peeled
3 medium onions, sliced
4 Roma tomatoes, peeled
1 head escarole, chopped
375 milliliters Chardonnay
   (1/2 bottle)
2 pinches salt
1/2 cup Italian parsley, chopped
1 clove garlic, chopped

> Along with a glass of Casa Larga Reserve Chardonnay, this soup is very hearty fare on a cold winter day.

Take the chicken breasts or cut up chicken and soak in cold water with the apple cider vinegar and salt for about 1/2 hour.

Meanwhile take an 8 quart cooking pot and fill with cold water and a tablespoon of salt. Place on stove and bring to a starting boil, rinse the chicken that has been soaking and put in the cooking pot and boil for approximately 10 minutes. Remove from heat, remove chicken from pot, rinse and set aside in clean dish or pan. Discard the water from the pot, wash the pot, fill with water and bring to a starting boil again. Submerge the chicken and bring to a slow boil. Place all of the vegetables in the pot and let simmer for twenty minutes.

Take out the chicken, rinse under cold water and remove the skin. Remove chicken from the bone. The meat should remove easily from the bone. Discard the bones and the skin. Rinse chicken again and place back in the boiling pot to cook for about one hour. As the soup is boiling, skim the foam from the top and discard.

When the carrots and celery are soft, soup should be done. Add the Chardonnay and let simmer about 10 minutes more.

Remove from the stove, place a strainer on top of another large pot and strain the chicken soup into the strainer so that all the food is left in the strainer and the clear bouillon has gone in the pot. Serve hot.

NOTE: If you prefer to leave all the meat and vegetables in the soup, instead of a clear broth, then cut up carrots, celery and chicken into small pieces. You might also add some soup pasta.

Per serving: 60 Calories; 0g Fat (6% calories from fat); 1g Protein; 8g Carbohydrate; 0mg Cholesterol; 861mg Sodium

NOTES

_____

_____

_____

_____

_____

_____

_____

Nine Bean Soup

From L. Mawby Vineyards, Michigan

Serves 12

2 cups dried beans,*
   sort and wash
2 tablespoons salt
3 pounds ham, one piece
1 medium onion, diced
1 large carrot, grated
5 cloves garlic, diced
1 tablespoon dried parsley
1 teaspoon caraway seed
1 cup dry white wine

Another hearty winter soup from the Northern Michigan wine country. L. Mawby Vignoles is an excellent choice with this meal.

   *9-Bean prepackaged mixes are available at most specialty food stores.
   After washing dried beans, place in large bowl and just cover them with water. Add salt, stir and let sit overnight.
   Next day: Drain bean mix, rinse once and cover with fresh water.
   In large pot, cover the ham piece with water and add onion, celery, carrot, garlic, parsley and caraway. Bring to a boil; simmer for 1 hour.
   Add bean mix with liquid plus wine. Return to a boil, then simmer for 3 hours until beans are tender.
   Cut up ham and serve with finished soup.

Per serving: 227 Calories; 12g Fat (52% calories from fat); 20g Protein; 5g Carbohydrate; 65mg Cholesterol; 2610mg Sodium

NOTES

_____

_____

_____

_____

_____

P's Leek & Potato Soup

From L. Mawby Vineyards, Michigan

Serves 10

4 cups water
1 cup dry white wine
2 large chicken bouillon cubes
2 cubes vegetable bouillon
2 cups leeks, diced
1 medium onion, diced
3 stalks celery, diced
5 medium potatoes, diced
15 ounces cannellini beans
1 teaspoon salt
4 tablespoons chives, chopped
2 cups kale, chopped

A classic soup, Northern Michigan style with L. Mawby Vignoles wine.

Bring water and wine to a boil. Add bouillon cubes and simmer to dissolve. Add leeks and onion, simmer. Add celery and potatoes, simmer for 15-20 minutes.

Pour 1 1/2 cups of soup into blender with beans and puree. Return puree to remaining soup and add salt, chives and kale. Blend mixture and heat 5-10 minutes.

Garnish with chopped chives.

Per serving: 246 Calories; 1g Fat (6% calories from fat); 13g Protein; 43g Carbohydrate; 1mg Cholesterol; 699mg Sodium

NOTES

_____

_____

_____

_____

_____

Pumpkin Soup

From Lakeshore Winery, Finger Lakes, New York

Serves 8

2 tablespoons margarine
2 small onions, finely chopped
1 carrot, finely chopped
1 large white potato, finely chopped
2 cloves garlic, finely chopped
1 1/2 teaspoons coriander, powdered
1 1/2 teaspoons cumin seed, powdered
4 cups chicken broth
1 can pumpkin (16 ounce size)
1/2 cup dry red wine
salt and Tabasco to taste

This recipe combines French and American harvest celebration traditions by opening a bottle of Lakeshore Winery Nouveau wine with the meal.

Melt margarine in a medium saucepan or wok. Add the vegetables, coriander and cumin. Saute the vegetables in the margarine until the onions are tender, about 5 minutes. Add one cup of the broth and simmer for 20 minutes. Puree mixture in a blender until smooth. Stir in pumpkin, wine, remaining chicken broth, Tabasco and salt. Heat through, but do not boil.

Per serving: 74 Calories; 2g Fat (33% calories from fat); 6g Protein; 5g Carbohydrate; 1mg Cholesterol; 936mg Sodium

NOTES

_____

_____

_____

_____

_____

_____

_____

Shrimp and Scallop Chowder from the Microwave

From Reif Estate Winery, Ontario

Serves 4

4 tablespoons butter
1/4 cup flour
1 1/2 cups milk
1/2 cup dry white wine
1 teaspoon garlic, minced
1 teaspoon salt
1/2 teaspoon white pepper
1/2 teaspoon cayenne pepper
1/2 teaspoon paprika
1 teaspoon Worcestershire sauce
3 tablespoons onions, chopped
1/2 cup fresh mushrooms, chopped
8 ounces cooked shrimp
12 ounces scallops
1 tablespoon green onion, chopped

Lovely as a soup appetizer course or serve over green noodles for a special luncheon or supper dish. Best enjoyed with a glass of Reif Estate Chardonnay Reserve.

In a 2-quart microwave-safe bowl, melt butter for 40 seconds on 100% power. Add flour, stirring until smooth. Gradually add milk, stirring thoroughly with whisk. Microwave uncovered for 3-4 minutes at 100% power.

When the mixture thickens, stir in wine, garlic, salt, pepper, cayenne pepper and Worcestershire sauce.

In a microwave-proof casserole, combine mushrooms and onions and microwave on 100% power for 3 minutes. Add them to the sauce, along with the cooked shrimp and scallops.

Cover and microwave on 70% power for approximately 8 minutes. Stir every 2 minutes. Let stand 3 minutes.

Garnish with paprika and chopped green onions.

Per serving: 344 Calories; 16g Fat (44% calories from fat); 31g Protein; 14g Carbohydrate; 182mg Cholesterol; 1001mg Sodium

Smoked Sausage Chowder

From Fox Run Vineyards, Finger Lakes, New York

Serves 6

1/2 pound sausage links
2 tablespoons butter
1/3 cup onion, chopped
1 cup celery, chopped
1 cup milk
1 cup beef bouillon
1/4 cup flour
1/4 teaspoon pepper
1 cup potatoes, cooked and cubed
1 cup lima beans, cooked

A hearty soup course
complemented by
Fox Run Pinot Noir or
Fox Trot Red.

Brown sausage links, remove and chop into bite sized pieces and set aside.
Add butter to saute pan or saucepan. Saute onion and celery until soft.
Mix in flour and milk until smooth. Add bouillon, sausage and remaining
ingredients (feel free to add 1/4 cup of dry red wine, if you like). Mix well,
simmer 10-15 minutes.

*Per serving: 343 Calories; 21g Fat (54% calories from fat); 13g Protein; 26g
Carbohydrate; 41mg Cholesterol; 592mg Sodium*

NOTES

_____

_____

_____

_____

_____

_____

Solera Mushroom Soup

From St. Julian Wine Co., Michigan

Serves 6

3 tablespoons, butter
1 teaspoon oil
1 pound mushrooms, chopped
3 tablespoons onion, chopped
1 tablespoon flour
1/2 cup cream sherry
3 1/4 cups beef broth
1 teaspoon fresh thyme, minced
1/4 teaspoon garlic powder
1/4 teaspoon fresh parsley, minced
1/4 teaspoon ground black pepper
1/2 teaspoon mustard powder
1/2 cup skim milk
1/2 cup half and half
2 teaspoons carrots, shredded, optional

The key to this soup is St. Julian's award-winning Solera Cream Sherry.

In a large saucepan, heat butter and oil over medium heat, add mushrooms and onions and saute for seven minutes.

Sprinkle the flour over the mixture, mix well. Blend in the cream sherry and cook for one minute.

Transfer this mixture to a blender and puree.

Pour the broth in blender. Add the thyme, garlic powder, parsley, mustard powder and black pepper. Blend this with the mushroom puree.

Return the soup to the saucepan and over medium high heat stir in skim milk and half and half. Warm the soup thoroughly, but do not bring it to a boil. Serve the soup with shredded carrots or a garnish of your choice.

Per serving: 158 Calories; 11g Fat (59% calories from fat); 9g Protein; 8g Carbohydrate; 24mg Cholesterol; 946mg Sodium

NOTES

_____

_____

Spicy Shrimp Salad

From St. Julian Wine Co., Michigan

Serves 6

1 1/2 pounds cooked shrimp,
  peeled and deveined
6 Roma tomatoes, quartered
1 head romaine lettuce, cut to bite size
1 each avocado, peel, cut to eighths
2 eggs or egg substitute
2 tablespoons Italian salad dressing
1 teaspoon dry mustard
1/4 teaspoon cumin
1/4 teaspoon paprika
1/4 teaspoon chili powder
1/2 teaspoon tabasco sauce
1/2 teaspoon salt
1/2 teaspoon black pepper
1/2 teaspoon red pepper
1 1/2 cups Canola oil

> A chilled glass of St. Julian Michigan Chardonnay would be a perfect accompaniment to this summer salad.

Divide the shrimp, tomatoes, lettuce and avocado on 6 chilled serving plates.

Place the eggs, salad dressing, and all spices in food processor. Process briefly. With motor running, slowly pour oil through feed tube and process until smooth. Top the salad with dressing.

Per serving: 718 Calories; 64g Fat (79% calories from fat); 28g Protein; 10g Carbohydrate; 282mg Cholesterol; 509mg Sodium

NOTES

_____

_____

_____

_____

Strawberry Wine Soup

From Fenn Valley Vineyards, Michigan

Serves 4

3 cups strawberries
1 1/2 cups white wine, semi-dry
1/4 cup sugar
2 tablespoons cornstarch
2 tablespoons water
2 tablespoons orange liqueur
    or amaretto

This recipe may be varied with peaches and amaretto or with raspberries and cassis. Enjoy all versions with a glass of Fenn Valley Riesling.

Mix cornstarch and water to form a paste.

Combine wine, berries and sugar in a saucepan. Bring to a boil and simmer 5 minutes. Add cornstarch mixture and cook until thick and clear. When cool, puree in food processor. Add liqueur. Chill. Serve in wine glasses or dessert dishes, topped with mint leaves or whipped cream.

(If using raspberries, increase sugar to 1/2 cup. With peaches, 3/4 cup of blueberries may be folded in just before chilling).

Per serving: 182 Calories; 0g Fat (3% calories from fat); 1g Protein; 27g Carbohydrate; 0mg Cholesterol; 6mg Sodium

NOTES

Sugar Shack Chili

From L. Mawby Vineyards, Michigan

Serves 12

1 1/2 cups bacon, fried crisp
2 quarts tomato sauce
1 small onion, chopped
5 medium shallots, chopped
1 cup Jerusalem artichokes, diced
15 ounces kidney beans
2 cups potato puree
2 cups dry red wine
2 tablespoons dried parsley
1 tablespoon thyme
1 tablespoon oregano
3 tablespoons chili powder
4 tablespoons maple sugar

A good hearty meal enjoyed during the early spring maple syrup harvest. L. Mawby Foch wine is our choice.

Combine all ingredients in pot. Heat to boiling, then simmer for 45 minutes to 1 hour.

Per serving: 408 Calories; 16g Fat (35% calories from fat); 21g Protein; 43g Carbohydrate; 25mg Cholesterol; 1539mg Sodium

NOTES

_____

_____

_____

_____

_____

_____

Vegetables

Baked Beans in Cider

From Old Firehouse Winery, Ohio

Serves 10

4 cups dried navy beans
3 cups apple cider or apple wine
1/2 pound salt pork
1 large onion, peeled
dry mustard
1/2 cup molasses
1 tablespoon salt

The Old Firehouse Winery recommends their Adam's Apple Cider for these "sure to please" baked beans.

Pick over, wash then cover the beans in cold water. Soak for 12 hours.

Drain the beans and place in a saucepan with the cider or wine. Bring to a boil and continue boiling for 1/2 hour. Garnish the bottom of an earthenware bean pot with about half the salt pork, cutting the remaining pork into slices for on top. Turn the beans and cider liquid into the bean pot. Roll the whole onion in dry mustard and bury it in the middle of the beans. Pour the molasses over all. Place the rest of the salt pork strips over the top and add enough hot water to cover. Salt and place cover on pot.

Bake 4 to 6 hours in a slow oven of 250 degrees F., checking every hour after the third. An hour before the beans are done, uncover the pot and add water if the beans seem too dry.

Per serving: 495 Calories; 19g Fat (35% calories from fat); 20g Protein; 62g Carbohydrate; 20mg Cholesterol; 1035mg Sodium

NOTES

_____

_____

_____

_____

_____

Barley Mushroom Ring

From Bowers Harbor Vineyards, Michigan

Serves 8

1 1/2 cups barley, dry
4 1/2 cups water
3/4 teaspoon salt
4 tablespoons butter
2/3 pound mushrooms, sliced
2 tablespoons parsley, chopped
1 clove garlic, minced
1 teaspoon salt
1/8 teaspoon pepper
1/4 teaspoon marjoram
1/4 cup butter
1/4 cup dry white wine

A wonderful vegetable dish with a generous glass of Bowers Harbor Vineyards Chardonnay from the Old Mission Peninsula.

Place barley, salt and 4 1/2 cups of water in saucepan. Bring to boil, cover and simmer for approximately 1 hour or until tender.

Melt butter, add mushrooms, parsley, garlic, salt, pepper and marjoram. Saute 5 minutes. Add 1/4 cups of butter and wine, heat.

Drain barley, combine with mushroom mixture. Pour into greased 6-cup ring mold or casserole. If ring mold is used place mold in pan of water.

Bake at 350 degrees F. for 45 minutes.

Per serving: 240 Calories; 12g Fat (46% calories from fat); 5g Protein; 28g Carbohydrate; 31mg Cholesterol; 596mg Sodium

NOTES

_____

_____

_____

_____

_____

Carmelized Onion

From Bowers Harbor Inn and Chateau Chantal, Michigan

Serves 2

1/2 large onion, julienned
1/8 cup sugar
1 teaspoon cracked black pepper

The sweetness level of these onions match beautifully with Chateau Chantal's Semi-Dry Riesling.

Lightly coat onion strips with sugar and pepper.
Place strips on non-stick pan in 350 degrees F. oven until brown.

Per serving: 58 Calories; 0g Fat (1% calories from fat); 0g Protein; 15g Carbo-hydrate; 0mg Cholesterol; 138mg Sodium

NOTES

RECIPES FROM THE WINERIES

Carole's Sauteed Mushrooms

From Lemon Creek Winery, Michigan

Serves 8

2 pounds button mushrooms, washed
8 tablespoons butter, sliced pieces
1/2 cup dry white wine, Seyval Blanc

A great recipe for morels or any other fresh mushroom. Serve as a vegetable dish or as an accompaniment to fish or steak with Lemon Creek Seyval Blanc - Dry.

Clean mushrooms, remove stems and save. You may slice large mushrooms or use small ones whole.

Melt butter in a large saute pan. Saute caps and stems in butter for 10 minutes. Add wine and saute 10 minutes longer.

Season with salt and pepper (optional).

Per serving: 138 Calories; 12g Fat (77% calories from fat); 2g Protein; 6g Carbohydrate; 31mg Cholesterol; 599mg Sodium

NOTES

_____

_____

_____

_____

_____

_____

_____

Classic Sauerkraut

From Fenn Valley Vineyards, Michigan

Serves 10

64 ounces sauerkraut, plain
1/4 cup brown sugar, optional
1 medium onion, chopped
1 large potato, grated w/skin
1 bottle white wine, semi-dry
12 juniper berries crushed
1 teaspoon caraway seeds, optional
1 teaspoon salt
1/2 teaspoon fresh ground pepper

Don't even think of serving this recipe with less than 8 hours of oven time. The secret is the slow baking and Fenn Valley Riesling.

Place all ingredients in a large non-metallic baking bowl and mix thoroughly. Bake for at least 8 hours at 225 degrees F., adding water as needed. Stir every two hours.

A bratwurst or piece of pork tenderloin may be added the last hour of cooking for added flavor. If adding meat, raise oven temperature to 350 degrees F. while cooking the meat.

Per serving: 60 Calories; 0g Fat (4% calories from fat); 2g Protein; 13g Carbohydrate; 0mg Cholesterol; 1470mg Sodium

NOTES

_____

_____

_____

_____

_____

_____

_____

Liebestrauben Glazed Carrots

From Warner Vineyards, Michigan

Serves 2

1 cup fresh carrots, julienned
1 tablespoon brown sugar
1 tablespoon butter
1/3 cup semi-dry white wine
1/3 cup water

Warner's popular Liebestrauben wine is the wine of choice for this vegetable side dish.

Melt butter in a sauce pan, add brown sugar, wine, water and carrots. Bring to a boil, cover and simmer for about 15 or 20 minutes.

Remove cover and continue cooking until carrots are tender, but still crisp, and most of the liquid has boiled off leaving only the butter glaze.

Per serving: 88 Calories; 6g Fat (57% calories from fat); 1g Protein; 9g Carbohydrate; 15mg Cholesterol; 78mg Sodium

NOTES

_____

_____

_____

_____

_____

_____

_____

_____

Tofu Veggie Kebabs

From Chateau Chantal, Michigan

Serves 4

1 pound tofu, firm 1" cubes
1 cup Chardonnay
1/2 cup Tamari soy sauce
1/2 cup olive oil
1 tablespoon garlic, minced
2 teaspoons ground ginger
1/8 teaspoon cayenne pepper
1 large onion, quartered
1 each green, red and yellow peppers,
    halved and quartered

Enjoy this veggie grill on a bed
of rice or wrapped in a warmed
tortilla shell and served with
Chateau Chantal Chardonnay.

Combine wine, soy sauce, olive oil, garlic, ginger and cayenne pepper to form a marinade. Marinde tofu and peppers (any grillable vegetables cut to bite size will work) for at least 45 minutes or overnight.

Impale ingredients on skewers; because of the delicate nature of tofu it is best to cradle each cube in either a section of onion or pepper.

Grill or broil until lightly browned, turning once.

Per serving: 396 Calories; 33g Fat (79% calories from fat); 13g Protein; 7g Carbohydrate; 0mg Cholesterol; 1769mg Sodium

NOTES

_____

_____

_____

_____

_____

_____

Vignoles Veggies

From L. Mawby Vineyards, Michigan

Serves 8

4 tablespoons butter
3 small onions, chopped
1 cup dry white wine
3 tablespoons flour
1 cup milk
1/4 teaspoon salt
1/8 teaspoon white pepper
1/8 teaspoon onion powder
1 tablespoon sugar
1 1/4 cups fresh carrots, julienned
1 cup green peas, fresh or frozen
1 cup cauliflower florets

This versatile recipe can be served over baked potato, pasta, pork tenderloin seared in butter or in individual pastry shells. But, always offer a glass of L. Mawby Vignoles.

Steam vegetables and set aside.

Saute onions in butter until transparent. Add wine and simmer to reduce by half. Blend in flour a little at a time until mixture is thick. Remove from heat to cool a bit. Slowly pour milk in until mixture will blend freely without lumps. Return to heat briefly.

Add salt, pepper, onion powder and sugar. Blend well and remove from heat. Add steamed veggies to sauce and gently stir to coat well. Taste and correct seasoning if necessary.

Transfer mixture to top of double boiler and simmer until veggies are heated thoroughly. Serves 8 as a side dish or 6 as a main dish over meat.

Per serving: 141 Calories; 7g Fat (50% calories from fat); 3g Protein; 13g Carbohydrate; 19mg Cholesterol; 357mg Sodium

NOTES

_____

_____

_____

_____

Ingredient Substitutions

Allspice = ground cinnamon, cloves and nutmeg in equal parts to equal total amount of allspice

Arrowroot (as a thickener), 1 1/12 tsp. = 1 Tbs. flour

Baking powder, 1 tsp. = 1/4 tsp. baking soda + 5/8 tsp. cream of tartar or (a rising equivalent) = 1/4 tsp. baking soda + 1/2 cup buttermilk or yogurt or 1/4 tsp. baking soda + 1/4 to 1/2 cup molasses

Basil = oregano

Bread crumbs, dry, 1 cup = 3/4 cup finely crumbled crackers or wheat germ or cereal

Broth, chicken or beef, 1 cup = 1 bouillon cube or 1 envelope of instant broth + 1 cup water

Brown sugar, 1 cup = 1 cup sugar + 1/4 cup molasses

Butter or margarine, 1 cup = 1 cup vegetable shortening + 1/2 tsp. salt

Buttermilk, 1 cup = 1 cup yogurt or 1 cup whole milk + 1 Tbs. lemon juice or vinegar (let stand 5 min.)

Caraway seeds = anise seeds

Cayenne pepper, ground = ground chili peppers

Celery seeds = celery tops, minced

Chervil = parsley or tarragon

Chicken = veal, turkey

Chocolate, unsweetened, 1 oz. = 3 Tbs. cocoa + 1 Tbs. butter or fat

Chocolate, semi-sweet, 1 oz. = 3 Tbs. unsweetened cocoa + 2 Tbs. water + 1 tsp. sugar

Cornstarch (for thickening), 1 Tbs. = 2 Tbs. all-purpose flour

Corn syrup (light), 1 cup = 1 1/4 cups granulated sugar + 1/3 cup water (not for baking)

Cream cheese, 8 oz. = 8 oz. yogurt cheese or Neufchatel cheese

Cream, half-and half, 1 cup = 1 1/2 Tbs. butter + 7/8 cup milk

Cream, whipping, 1 cup = 1/3 cup butter + 3/4 cup milk

Egg (for baking), 1 egg = 2 egg whites

Egg yolks (for thickening), 2 yolks = 1 whole egg

Fennel = anise seed

Flour, all-purpose, 1 cup = 1 cup whole-wheat flour minus 2 Tbs.

Flour, white, 1 cup = 1 cup cornmeal or 5/8 cup potato flour or 1 cup minus 2 Tbs. rice flour or 1 1/4 cup rye flour or 13/16 cup gluten flour

Flour (as thickening agent), 1 Tbs. = 1 1/2 tsp. cornstarch (or potato, rice, arrowroot starch) or 1 Tbs. quick-cooking tapioca or 1 Tbs. rice flour or 1 Tbs. corn flour

Fresh herbs, 1 Tbs. = 1/3 tsp. dried

Garlic, 1 clove = 1/8 tsp. garlic powder

Ginger, raw, 1 Tbs. = 1/8 tsp. powdered

Green pepper = red or yellow pepper

Ground beef = ground pork, veal or lamb

Honey, 1 cup = 1 1/4 cup sugar + 1/4 cup liquid

Ketchup or chili sauce, 1/2 cup = 1/2 cup tomato sauce + 2 Tbs. sugar + 1 Tbs. vinegar + 1/8 tsp. each of ground cloves and allspice

Lemon juice, 1 Tbs. = 1 to 3 Tbs. vinegar

Lemon, grated rind, 1 tsp. = 1/2 tsp. lemon extract

Mace = nutmeg

Maple sugar, 1 Tbs. = 1 Tbs. granulated sugar

Maple sugar, 1/2 cup = 1 cup maple syrup

Marjoram = oregano

Milk, whole, 1 cup = $1/2$ cup evaporated milk + $1/2$ cup water or $1/4$ cup dry whole milk + $7/8$ cup water

Mushrooms, fresh, 8 oz. = one 6 oz. can mushrooms, drained

Mustard, prepared, 1 Tbs. = $1/2$ tsp. dried mustard

Nutmeg = mace

Nuts, 1 Tbs. = 1 Tbs. Grape Nuts cereal

Onion, 1 small = 1 Tbs. instant minced onion

Oregano, 1 tsp. = 1 $1/4$ tsp. dried marjoram

Ricotta cheese, 1 cup = 1 cup cottage cheese + 1 Tbs. skim milk blended until smooth

Sage = thyme

Sour cream, 1 cup = 3 Tbs. butter + $7/8$ cup buttermilk or yogurt or 1 cup plain yogurt

Sugar, 1 cup = 1 cup honey or corn syrup (omit $1/4$ cup of the liquid if used in a recipe)

Sugar, powdered, 1 $1/3$ cup = 1 cup granulated sugar

Tapioca (for thickening), 1 Tbs. = 1 Tbs. flour

Tomatoes, 1 cup packed = $1/2$ cup tomato sauce and $1/2$ cup water

Tomato paste, 1 Tbs. = 1 Tbs. ketchup

Vinegar, 1 tsp. = 2 tsp. lemon juice

Whipped cream, 1 $3/4$ cups = 1 can well-chilled evaporated milk + 3 Tbs. lemon juice, whipped until stiff

Worcestershire sauce, 1 tsp. = 1 Tbs. soy sauce + dash garlic powder + dash cayenne

Yogurt, 1 cup = 1 cup buttermilk

Substitutions compiled and supplied by Master Cook Deluxe, a software product of Sierra-on-Line.

Great Lakes Contributing Wineries

ARBOR HILL GRAPERY
6461 Route 64
Bristol Springs
Naples, NY 14512
(716) 374-2406
(800) 554-7553

Wine isn't the only delicious commodity made from grapes. And you'll never know how extensive the product line can be until you step into the Arbor Hill Grapery or leaf through the Grapery's Gift Catalog. John and Katie Braham make not only wine, but they also produce a wonderful array of wine sauces (dessert and barbecue), preserves, jellies, flavored vinegars, mustards, award-winning dressings and even the area's famous "grape pie filling." They also put together an endless array of gift crates and custom-made baskets to be shipped to customers all over the U.S. and Canada.

Arbor Hill food products can be found in many winery gift shops throughout the Finger Lakes or you can write or call for the Arbor Hill catalog. But the real fun is visiting the Grapery and experiencing the delight of exploring the shelves for a delicious treat.

Easy and Elegant Trifle
Fruit Dip
Wine Sauce Barbecue (for Beef)
Wine Sauce Barbecue (for Poultry)
Hot 'n' Sweet Barbecue
Sherried Flank Steak
Burgundy Chicken

BOWERS HARBOR VINEYARDS
2896 Bowers Harbor Road
Old Mission Peninsula
Traverse City, MI 49684
(616) 223-7615

Jack Stegenga opened a stockbroker's office in Traverse City, Michigan in 1969 and since that time has extended himself to include additional careers as a restaurateur and rancher. In the 80's his restaurant interest led him to the wine country of Germany where a new passion began to take seed. The Stegenga's farm/ranch was transformed into five acres of vineyards featuring premium Chardonnay and Riesling grapes. Within a short time Bowers Harbor Vineyards gained recognition and popularity by earning competitive awards for their wines.

Bowers Harbor has a charming tasting room at the vineyard site. It is a beautiful drive out the Old Mission Peninsula with stunning bay views and picturesque rolling acreage of orchards and thriving vinifera grapes. As the Stegengas so accurately express, "A wine-tasting trip to Bowers Harbor Vineyards is a gift to the senses."

Wasabi Sauce
Herb-Crusted Salmon
Country Chicken Piccata
Barley Mushroom Ring
Caramelized Onion

BUCCIA VINEYARDS
518 Gore Road
Conneaut, OH 44030
(216) 593-5976

Sometimes visiting a winery is so much fun you don't want to leave. Fred and Joanna Buccia make it very difficult to leave their winery grounds by providing not only a rustic tasting room, a cordial staff and excellent wines, but also a romantic "getaway" bed & breakfast, complete with private hot tubs and the serenity of a country setting.

The Buccia family describes a visit to the winery as a "memorable outing." They invite visitors to "bring your family and enjoy a picturesque scene, ranging from the blue skies and intriguing vineyards of luscious deep burgundy grapes to the golden glow of the white grapes. Prepare your palate with alluring cheeses and breads, sip fine wines, stroll the spacious grounds or relax at one of many arbor-covered picnic tables. Children are welcome at the winery and non-alcoholic beverages are available for them." Now, that's a difficult invitation to turn down!

Spinach-Artichoke Dip

CASA LARGA VINEYARDS
27 Emerald Hill Circle
Fairport, NY 14450
(716) 223-8899

This architectural award-winning winery is a brilliant combination of old world tradition and charm with state-of-the-art technology designed for contemporary use and efficiency.

The Casa Larga structure with its old-world bell tower and piazza, dramatic floor-to-ceiling windows, Italian marble and vaulted ceilings is so impressive that it is difficult to talk about anything else. But, once you enter the strikingly attractive retail room your attention is immediately diverted to an extensive array of eye-catching merchandise and wines of notable quality.

The effort Colaruotolo devoted to the construction of his illustrious building is also reflected in the quality of his wines. All the vineyards are tended by hand to produce a number of award-winners.

"We have always felt that our winery has been a place for people to come and enjoy the building and grounds as much as the wine," says General Manager John Colaruotolo. It is worth the trip to Casa Larga Vineyards just to see the masterpiece that Mr. "C" built...and to drink his wine.

Mrs. C's Classic Pork Loin Chops
Mrs. C's Chicken Chardonnay Soup

CASTEL GRISCH ESTATE WINERY
3380 County Route 28
Watkins Glen, NY 14891
(607) 535-9614

A warm, friendly feeling is very prevalent at the Castel Grisch Estate, situated on a high slope overlooking Watkins Glen and the southern end of Seneca Lake.

The continental ambiance of the estate is preserved by a well-trained staff that carries on the European traditions of fine estate-produced wines, tastefully distinct cuisine and elegant overnight accommodations.

This scenic hillside estate is truly a celebration of wine, food and friends all blended together to enhance the pleasure of their guests. The Castel is the ideal spot for wedding receptions, private parties, corporate meetings and family gatherings, not to mention a great meal for two in the Swiss chalet decor of the restaurant.

The good life at the Castel includes occasional seven course/seven wine gourmet dinners and an Oktoberfest celebration the last weekend in October,

as well as other Seneca Lake Wine Trail events. Excellent limited production/ estate bottled wines, a romantic room and superb apple strudel...what else is there in life?
Fondue for Two

CEDAR SPRINGS WINES
at Eastman's Market
Highway 3 (just west of Blenheim), Ontario
(519) 676-8008

The Cedar Springs Vineyards and Tasting Room are a division of London Winery, Ltd. The Cedar Springs location is a casual stop as it sits next to a roadside market and entertains its visitors with a vineyard tour and then a tasting in a converted 10,000 gallon redwood barrel aptly named "The Barrel Room."
The Cedar Springs estate supplies the premium vinifera and French hybrid grapes for the winery's Proprietor's Reserve wines that have achieved the VQA (Vintners Quality Alliance) designation.
Mama Mia's Chili
Luscious Lemony Scallops
Orange Beef Stir-Fry

CHALET DEBONNÉ VINEYARDS
7734 Doty Road
Madison, OH 44057
(216) 466-3485

Chalet Debonné is one of Ohio's most "happening" wineries. Besides being an innovative leader in the production of fine quality wines from the Lake Erie Region, Chalet Debonné is a "hot spot" for fun and entertainment from May to September. What other winery do you know of that on any given weekend you may find an exhibition of model airplanes or antique steam engines, a Hot-Air Balloon Festival or kite flying, one of many diversified summer concerts, or a very unique "pet day" with judging from cutest to ugliest pet? This kind of activity and excitement progresses to Labor Day weekend with "Family Fun Day" with all sorts of games and activities for the entire family.
The Debevc's family commitment to quality is obvious when you visit their winery and sample their wine. It's true what they say about Chalet Debonné, "Fine wines distinctively separate from the bunch."
Not Enough Shrimp Dip

CHATEAU CHANTAL
15900 Rue de Vin
Old Mission Peninsula
Traverse City, MI 49684
(616) 223-4110

The picturesque landscape settings of the Old Mission Peninsula are personified at the majestic estate of Chateau Chantal, which features northern Michigan's only bed and breakfast winery. The winery site straddles a ridge near the northern end of the peninsula. Nearly every part of the property offers stunning views of either side of Lake Michigan's Grand Traverse Bay.

The area has long been a coveted secret as a favorite summer and winter vacation spot. The peninsula's primary agricultural industry is cherry and grape-growing. Chateau Chantal has been designed not only to physically fit within the scenic environment, but also to offer a quality product line and lodging that are in keeping with the area's growing reputation for fine foods, exceptional hospitality and superb wines. From the vineyard, to the winery, to the tasting room, a feeling of being one with nature is strongly evident in this most breathtaking of settings.

Tofu Veggie Kebabs

CHATEAU DES CHARMES
1025 York Road
St. Davids, Ontario L0S 1P0
(905) 262-4210

There is no winery structure in Ontario that is more majestic than the imposing edifice at Château des Charmes. Easily accessible off the Q.E.W. highway, this magnificent new building is set within an immaculate 85-acre vineyard and seductively beckons all who venture near.

From the moment you pass through the distinctive entryway, you know you are viewing a winery masterpiece. A huge glass chandelier sparkles in the light above the French door entrance to the "Theatre" where an informative 15-minute video presentation takes place. Next, admiring visitors cross the grand foyer bound for a walking tour of the state-of-the-art winemaking facilities, the barrel aging room and then finish in the tasting room dominated by the presence of an exquisite oak wine bar.

As the folks at Château des Charmes proudly state, "Our new château is a modern rendition of an old world tradition." And, it's an awesome accomplishment!

Veal Medallions with Herbs and Cream Sauce
Poulet D'Andree

CHATEAU GRAND TRAVERSE
12239 Center Road
Old Mission Peninsula
Traverse City, MI 49686
(616) 223-7355

What would motivate a successful businessman to risk his assets and venture into the precarious world of making wine in an area that all the "experts" said was too unpredictable? Edward O'Keefe quips, "Back in 1974, people must have thought I had more money than brains. They said the Northern Michigan climate could only be withstood by American hybrid grapes. I wanted to grow European Vinifera grapes and my research indicated that it could be done. I wanted to prove that world-class wine could be made in Michigan."

From that early commitment to plant primarily Riesling and Chardonnay grapes, Chateau Grand Traverse has continued to experiment with other varieties. Today, O'Keefe is happy about the red wine production of Pinot Noir and Merlot and particularly enthusiastic about the development of Gamay, a crisp, fruity red wine that in the last few years has become a tasting room favorite.

Sesame-Chutney Cheese Log
Champagne Blossom Punch

FENN VALLEY VINEYARDS
6130 122nd Ave.
Fennville, MI 49408
(800) 432-6265

A family love for home winemaking and an extensive research program brought the William Welsch family in 1973 to the little farm and orchard community of Fennville in southwest Michigan. Equipped with a degree in chemistry, the financial security of a successful building-supply company in Chicago and a wine-making son with a biology background, Welsch took on the odds against success in the wine business.

Doug Welsch has taken over the reigns as president from his father and plans on extensive growth in the family business. The Welsches are in the early stages of planning a restaurant to complement their banquet facility. By the year 2000 Fenn Valley Vineyards will not only offer visitors some award-winning wines made from Pinot Gris, Chancellor and Chardonel grapes, but may also be serving some of those wonderful Welsch family German recipes that are sampled by lucky folks who happen to stop by the winery on a special Wine & Food Weekend.

Garlic Spread
No-Fat Peach Dessert
Tropical Fruit Kebabs with Caramel Sauce
Low-Fat Mustard Dill Sauce
Tomato & Curry Sauce/Marinade
Baked Fish in Wine
Grilled Fish
Italian Stuffed Steak
Stuffed Pork Tenderloin
Chicken in Red Wine
Minted Pea Soup
Strawberry Wine Soup
Classic Sauerkraut

FERRANTE WINERY & RISTORANTE
5585 State Route 307
Geneva, OH 44041
(216) 466-VINO

Since 1937 the Ferrante family had transported the grapes from their vineyard in the Geneva area to their winery in Cleveland. In 1979, prompted by the growth of tourism along Interstate 90, the family built a spotless, modern facility at their vineyard location. The winery has grown to be one of the largest family-owned wineries in Ohio.

In 1989, the third generation of Ferrante children expanded the winery to include an Italian Ristorante. To the Ferrantes, and to most other Italian families, it is a natural progression to include food with wine. The restaurant is handsomely decorated and offers a sweeping, scenic view of the vineyards. It includes an open-air dining patio and provides a menu that is worth the trip by itself. If you would like to have your own private tasting of Ferrante wines, order one of the sampler selections with your meal.

The Ferrante Winery and Ristorante facility is a "must" stop as you visit the area. Call ahead to get the schedule of special events and activities sponsored by the winery.

Escalope of Veal Vidal
Linguine with Chardonnay Clam Sauce
Pollo Vino Al Lamponi (Chicken Raspberry)

FIRELANDS WINERY
917 Bardshar Road
Sandusky, OH 44870
(419) 625-5474

Firelands Winery is named for the region in which it is located. A twenty-five mile long area along the southern shore of Lake Erie, between Toledo and Cleveland. The name Firelands originated during the Revolutionary War when British troops raided and burned coastal towns in Connecticut. The destruction and fire was so devastating that many families were left with nothing. In compensation for their losses, citizens were allotted land from Connecticut's Western Reserve in northern Ohio. This area became known as The Firelands.

The Firelands Winery is located right in the middle of the popular tourist area of Northern Ohio known as "Vacationland." A visit to the winery is a wonderful treat any time of the year. The retail shop is full of unusual and interesting gift ideas and the video is one of the best-produced presentations on the area's colorful history and the magic of winemaking. Firelands Winery also offers special events and wine appreciation/cooking classes during the winter.

Jambalaya, Lake Erie Style
Poule au Pot (Chicken in a Pot)

FOX RUN VINEYARDS
670 Route 14
Pen Yan, NY 14527
(315) 536-4616

Scott Osborn, owner of Fox Run Vineyards, has worked from California to New York as a winemaker, cellarmaster, wine salesman, wine consultant and teacher. He has been described as a *bon vivant* who loves fine wine and food. Osborn also has a soft spot in his heart for animals as evidenced by the winery's adoption and fund-raising efforts for the Arctic Fox habitat at Rochester's Seneca Park Zoo. By all accounts, a man of this experience, compassion and zest for life, has to make good wine. Well, he does!

The Fox Run winery and tasting room was built around an old dairy barn. Complimentary tours take visitors throughout the building and into the vineyards, then back to the tasting bar and a dramatic view of Seneca Lake.

If you're looking for unusual wine-related items, here is where you'll find them. Fox Run has one of the most extensive gift shops in the Finger Lakes area with an array of items ranging from gourmet food products to grape-covered boxer shorts.

Wild Mushroom Sauté
White Bean Pasta Sauce
Black Bean Soup
Smoked Sausage Chowder

FRONTENAC POINT VINEYARD
9501 Route 89
Trumansburg, NY 14886
(607) 387-9619

Highway 89 is the Cayuga Wine Trail. Although the area is rural, the highway is very comfortable to travel and the green grape cluster signs along the way make it easy to spot the Cayuga Lake wineries with their beautiful views of the Lake.

One such scenic spot is the Frontenac Point Vineyard located on the western shore of Cayuga Lake just 12 miles north of Ithaca, New York. Proprietors Jim and Carol Doolittle have created a classic French setting in their winery tasting room and offer estate-grown wines ". . . in the French tradition of winemaking."

Frontenac Point Vineyard folks say all of their wines are produced by barrel fermentation, a vinification technique that complements wines with subtlety and complexity. They then age the wine in small oak barrels of both American and European origin until it's mature and ready for bottling. The results are very intriguing.

Venison or Beef Roast in Wine Sauce

FULKERSONS WINERY AND JUICE PLANT
5576 Route 14
Dundee, NY 14837
(607) 243-8270

As indicated by it's name, Fulkerson's Winery and Juice Plant is a slightly different kind of winery than you'll find along the Seneca Lake Winery Trail. As you drive up to Fulkerson's it looks very much like a country farm market. Well, it is. A farm market and a winery, as well.

Fulkerson's has been a family farm since 1805 and they established the winery in 1988. Home winemakers have become so dependent on them, however, that their business never made the complete transition to a tourist-oriented retail winery. The Fulkerson brochure, in fact, headlines "Join the many people who enjoy home winemaking and find out how rewarding and satisfying it is!"

Fulkerson's is an interesting stop along the Wine Trail, especially during harvest time, if for no other reason than just to see the juice plant in operation. While there, you can also try the wines of the Fulkerson's and take home some fresh farm produce as well.

Red Wine Jelly Dogs

GLENORA WINE CELLAR
5435 Route 14
Dundee, NY 14837
(607) 243-5511

There are a number of reasons why visitors to the Finger Lakes should not miss visiting the impressive Glenora Wine Cellars. First is the winery's emphasis on *méthode champenoise* (fermented in the bottle) sparkling wines. Glenora handcrafts these wines in the French tradition using only the classic varieties of Pinot Noir, Pinot Blanc and Chardonnay.

A second reason is the Wine Garden Cafe with a delicious array of luncheon and dinner entrees served on the covered patio just outside the tasting room. Visitors and locals alike fill the popular cafe every day during the summer season. It's worth the effort to call ahead and reserve your table. The food and the view tempts one to stay around until the next meal.

The final reason to visit the Glenora Wine Cellars and Garden Cafe is for the number of special events that are sponsored by the winery in their outdoor pavilion. Jazz concerts, a Lobster Festival and a German Festival are just a few of the popular activities that keep people coming back to the winery.

Choucroute Garnie

GOOD HARBOR VINEYARDS
Leland, MI 49653
(M-22 three miles south of Leland)
(616) 256-7165

Bruce Simpson is not the high-profile sort of winemaker seen making the speaking circuit these days. Simpson is very low-key and prefers to allow his popular Good Harbor wines to speak for themselves, especially when accompanied on the dinner table with freshwater fish and seafood.

Though Simpson professes to be a pure farmer and winemaker, he is generally credited for introducing one of Michigan's most successful marketing coups with the introduction of the best-selling "Trillium." This semi-dry, white wine blend of Seyval, Vignoles, Vidal and Riesling, with its colorful rendition of the Trillium flower on the label, brought instant recognition to retail shelves and overnight success for the winery.

The Good Harbor Winery is located right behind the family's Farm Market and Bakery. If your sense of smell allows you to pass by this location without stopping, then you'd better see a doctor about those sinus problems.

Venison Swiss Steak

Wine, Herb & Garlic-Marinated Leg of Lamb

HENRY OF PELHAM ESTATE WINERY
1469 Pelham Road
St. Catharines, Ontario L2R 6P7
(905) 684-8423

In 1794, Nicholas Smith was awarded a land grant in Canada for his dedicated service to the English crown. Smith guaranteed a family tradition and legacy for his land by fathering fourteen children. In 1842, his son Henry, known as Henry of Pelham in the official archives, built Henry Smith's Inn & Tollgate which served as a focal point for the community over the next 100 years.

Today, two additional descendants, Paul and Matthew Speck, have fully restored the old inn to house the Henry of Pelham winery tasting room, boutique and banquet facilities. Upon entering the downstairs tasting room one has the feeling of setting foot in an old English wine cellar. But in actuality, the lower level room was the kitchen for the original inn and visitors may still observe the same huge brick oven that baked bread for the customers upstairs.

During the busy summer months the estate is often the site for weekend barbecues, food and wine festivals and numerous other events where locals and tourists alike gather for good food, excellent wine and camaraderie.

Green Onion Crepes

Peach and Mascarpone Mousse in Phyllo

Poached Apples

Duck Breast in a Black Currant Glaze

HERITAGE WINE CELLARS
12162 East Main Rd. (Rte 20)
North East, PA 16428
(814) 725-8015

In 1833 Harvey Hall purchased the original 100 acre fruit farm that later became known as the Heritage Wine Cellars. His great-grandson, Kenneth Bostwick, converted the farm to grape production. Today, great-great-grandson Robert manages several farms totaling nearly 400 acres of vineyards.

Heritage Wine Cellars is located in a restored 18th century barn, nestled in the heart of the Lake Erie Wine Region. The black walnut wood framework is an impressive piece of farm architecture supported by 60 and 70 foot beams throughout the structure. Just walking into the hospitality room of the old barn, one gets a nostalgic feeling of a bygone era and a tradition that this family will not let die.

A visit to the Heritage Wine Cellars is a pleasing trip back in time and a sharing of a farm family's traditions. In fact, most days you'll find grandpa Bostwick in the tasting room ready and willing to share stories of the old days of farming in the Lake Erie Region while you sample the tasty fruits of his family's effort.

Dutch Apple Pork Chops
Raspberry Chicken a la Orange

HERNDER ESTATE WINERY
1607 8th Avenue
St. Catharines, Ontario L2R 6P7
(905) 684-3300

Some wineries have interesting histories, others have impressive facilities and yet others have wonderfully esthetic grounds. The Hernder Estate Winery has all of these and more. Approaching the winery on the horizon off Highway 8, one is awestruck by the striking presence of a massive 127 year old restored barn. As the picture unfolds, the larger-than-life scene becomes even more breathtaking with its expansive grounds of stocked ponds, manicured landscaping and stone-walled fences. The interior of this magnificent structure is just as impressive with a well-appointed tasting room/gift shop, hospitality room and an adjoining modern winery.

Continuing this extraordinary endeavor, already over seven years in the making, future plans call for a full-service restaurant, additions to the already beautiful outdoor panorama such as a covered bridge, gazebos, special public events and dozens of other marketing ideas that will call attention to the Hernder Winery and its wines.

Duck Liver Pate
Fresh-Thyme Roasted Cornish Game Hens
Grilled Garlic Shrimp Salad

HUNT COUNTRY VINEYARDS
4021 Italy Hill Road
Branchport, NY 14418
(315) 595-2821

In the early 1800's Aaron Hunt came to Yates County and purchased farmland on Keuka Lake near Branchport, New York. In 1973 Arthur and Joyce Hunt moved to the farm and became the sixth generation of Hunts to work the same land.

The winery was something of a necessity for the modern day Hunts. Back in 1973 when Hunt took over the farm from his uncle, grapes where fetching $440 a ton and life was grand. But by the mid-1980's the purchase price of grapes was down as low as $80 a ton and suddenly a farm crisis raised its ugly head. Hunt decided to take advantage of the 1976 Farm Winery Act and build a winery. The new state law allowed a "farm winery" to make and sell up to 150,000 gallons a year directly to consumers and retailers.

One of the most popular attractions at Hunt Country Vineyards is their annual Gourmet Harvest Festival the first weekend in October. It's a great family outing with fantastic gourmet food prepared by culinary students. Also featured are horse-drawn hayrides, pony rides, arts & crafts, a petting zoo and, of course, Hunt Country wines.

Grilled Chicken Moutard
Turkey Tetrazzini

INNISKILLIN WINES
R.R. 1 (on Line 3 off the Niagara Parkway)
Niagara-on-the-Lake, Ontario L0S 1J0
(905) 468-3554

The name Inniskillin is derived from an old Irish military regiment named the Inniskilling Fusiliers who served during the War of 1812.

Set in the middle of vineyards with an approaching drive lined with large wooden wine barrels, your expectations for a very special visit begin to rise as you enter the estate. The boutique is located in an old restored barn, but don't let the outside barnwood appearance fool you. The interior, which houses the retail shop, an art gallery loft and an accommodating staff, is of modern design and geared for contemporary retailing.

With a little planning you can also participate in one of the many special activities scheduled in the summer and fall, including chef demonstrations, artist exhibits and book signings. Inniskillin Winery is definitely a "must stop" along the scenic Niagara Parkway.

Iced Champagne Sabayon
Iced Pear Soufflé
Prawn and Pancetta Skewers with Chive Sauce
Veal Medallions with Wild Mushrooms

KITTLING RIDGE ESTATE WINES & SPIRITS
297 South Service Road
Grimsby, Ontario L3M 4E9
(905) 945-4330

With the international success of Ontario's Icewine, Kittling Ridge's owner John Hall decided to experiment with a blend of Icewine and brandy, an idea similar to the French Pineau de Charente which is a blend of white wine and Cognac. Hall recognized that the Icewine of the area was excellent and was receiving more recognition everyday, but everyone was making it and he felt it was a bit too sweet. To differentiate his Icewine from the rest of the pack, brandy was introduced to it. The outcome was a tasting room hit for "Icewine & Brandy." His next step was to create an *eau de vie* from Icewine and blend it back into the undistilled portion of the wine. The resulting sensation of "Icewine & Eau de Vie" serves as a superb apéritif or dessert wine that offers an intense fruit flavor without being syrupy sweet. It actually complements a meal of fresh shrimp, crab or lobster very nicely.

Hot Cranberry-Melba Cabernet Sauvignon
Flamboyant Pacific Snapper
Maple Mustard Chops
Canadian Maple Chicken
Roman Chicken Bastilla

L. MAWBY VINEYARDS
4519 South Elm Valley Road
Suttons Bay, MI 49682
(616) 271-3522

L. Mawby Vineyards is a small winery producing estate-grown *methode champenoise* (bottle-fermented) sparkling wines and full-bodied, Burgundian-style white table wines from twelve acres of vineyards on the hills near Suttons Bay on Michigan's Leelanau Peninsula.

Winemaker and owner Larry Mawby is a man of the earth and is dedicated to agriculture from grapes to the family orchards and most all natural farm products. Nature's bounty ends up on Mawby's table in a country-hearty and healthy form along with a bottle of one of his highly regarded wines and most likely a recalling of some English literature that has struck his fancy.

Morel Frattata
Baked Stuffed Lake Trout
Mother's Stew with a Twist
Roast Venison with Morels
Special Meat Loaf
Morel Mushrooms in Wine Sauce
Three Star Goulash
Vegetable Smothered Linguine
Winemaker's Spanish Rice
Chicken in a Pot
Autumn Celebration Bean Soup
Nine Bean Soup
P's Leek & Potato Soup
Sugar Shack Chili
Vignoles Veggies

LAKE MICHIGAN WINERY
US 41 (Calumet Ave. at 119 th St.)
Whiting, IN 46394
(219) 659-3501

The Lake Michigan Winery building is a unique structure of brick, concrete and steel beams that one may guess would house an art studio. Indeed art is the subject, albeit the art of making wine.

A tour of the winery takes you beneath the building and the typical moldy aroma of a wine cellar where nearly 10,000 gallons of wine are aged in stainless steel and oak vats. At the other end of the cellar is the scrubbed floor and polished stainless steel tanks of the actual working winery where sanitation is a top priority for making good wine.

At the end of the tour visitors are invited to taste the product and look through a variety of wine accessories available in the retail room. The inventory here ranges from numerous wine art items to exotic corkscrews and, of course, the ever-present T-shirt touting, in this case, "Indiana Wine - A Grape Idea."

Strawberry Chicken

LAKESHORE WINERY
5132 Route 89
Romulus, NY 14541
(315) 549-7075

Winemaker/owner John Backman conducts wine seminars in the Lakeshore Winery tasting room complete with a sample compliment of food. "It sets us apart from everybody else," explains Backman. "We spend time with our guests, get them to sit down, relax and have an enjoyable experience while we discuss wine and its marriage with food. It gets a little hectic on weekends, but the seminar format has become our trademark and people expect it."

Backman takes his visitors on a tasting tour of Lakeshore wines in the comfortable farm setting of his hospitality room. The presentation lasts about twenty minutes, but sometimes during the week folks stick around to ask questions and further discuss wine. It's all very casual and extremely informative as Backman tries to dispel the mystique of wine with food. His philosophy and advice to customers is, "Don't worry about which wine goes with which food. Just find a wine you like, and enjoy it."

Spaghetti Pretzels
Vegetarian Pate
Cherry Delight
Mustard Veggie Dip
Pasta Salad with Sun-Dried Tomato and Olive Pesto
Pumpkin Soup

LEELANAU WINE CELLARS
County Road 626
Omena, MI 49674
(616) 386-5201

The fastest-growing winemaking area in Michigan seems to be in the northwest region of the state. Contributing to this accelerated growth is the area's largest winery - Leelanau Wine Cellars, located on the Leelanau Peninsula.

The Leelanau tasting room offers more than a spectacular view of Grand Traverse Bay. A new blended wine at the change of each season is introduced much to the pleasure of Northern Michigan tourists and wine fanciers. The result of this new blending philosophy are wines that express the freedom of creativity and good taste. These seasonal offerings have been a contributing factor in Leelanau Wine Cellars' move from the seventh largest wine production facility in the state in 1987 to the second largest in 1994.

Just down the hill from the winery is a little cheese shop called the Leelanau

Cheese Company that offers some great "old world" cheeses made on location.

Green Fish Sauce
Poached Lake Michigan Trout
Beef Stew Leelanau
Country Veal
Spinach Lasagna
Traverse Bay Chicken

LEMON CREEK VINEYARDS
533 Lemon Creek Road
Berrien Springs, MI 49103
(616) 471-1321

Nearly twenty-five years ago, the Lemon family realized that the same lake-effect climate conditions of cool springtimes and warm autumns that were beneficial to their six generation fruit-growing business were also helpful for the cultivation of grapes. It was a natural progression to extend their farming efforts to include grape-growing.

As the demand for premium wine grapes developed, so did the Lemons' vineyard expansion. It wasn't until 1984, however, that brothers Tim, Jeff and Bob Lemon decided to open their own winery and diversify their production to include the marketing of wine during the winter months. Today, Lemon Creek is still a major supplier of premium grapes to a number of Michigan wineries as well as a prominent producer of wines under its own label.

Lemon Creek is, first and foremost, a multiple-fruit farm. The winery is small, but it has its advantages in quality control of production.

Summer Sangria
Wine Sauce for Fish
Cheryl's Scallops in Mustard Sauce
Poached Salmon
Carole's Sautéed Mushrooms

LONDON WINERY
540 Wharncliffe Road S.
London, Ontario N6J 2N5
(519) 686-8431

London Winery, Ltd. is one of oldest, largest and most successful family winery operations in Ontario, and has only recently opened its hallowed halls to the public. In 1993, the third generation Knowles brothers decided to allow tours of the winemaking facilities for the first time in its nearly 70-year history by building an impressive $1.5 million, 15,000 sq. ft. touring center adjacent to the winery.

Now that the family has graciously opened its doors, the stylish visitor's center has become a "must see" attraction with its decor of cherry wood, ceramic tile and exquisite antiques. Guests may now examine the history of the company, view winery memorabilia and take in a comprehensive explanation of vineyard management and winemaking in the audio-visual theater.

After sixty-some years, the low-profile London Winery has come to life to meet the challenge of contemporary marketing for the benefit of the consumer.

Icewine Truffles
London Curry Dip

LONZ WINERY
Middle Bass Island
Middle Bass, OH 43446
(419) 285-5411

Little did Peter Lonz realize in 1884 when he started producing wines on Middle Bass Island that his winery would become one of Ohio's premier tourist attractions. Aided by the construction of a magnificent Gothic winery building designed by George Lonz in 1934, tens of thousands of visitors have enjoyed a bottle of Lonz wine on the terrace overlooking the shimmering waters of Lake Erie dotted with boats of all sizes and types. Once summer kicks into full gear, the island "rocks" with a full schedule of live entertainment and special events. From sailboat racing and a 5K run, to a grape-stomping festival and barbecues, the action rarely stops.

Lonz is a perfect family venue with special family-oriented events on Wednesdays. Each day, playground and picnic facilities are available for everyone to enjoy. If you plan to visit the island winery, be sure to call ahead for the entertainment schedule and tour times.

Country Ham Holiday Meatballs
Great Lakes Vineyard Barbecue Sauce
Tournedos Madere (Sautéed Steak Filet with Maderia Glaze)

LUCAS VINEYARDS
3862 County Road 150
Interlaken, NY 14847
(607) 532-4825

It sounds like a strange (and busy) life, but Bill Lucas is a genuine tugboat captain in New York harbors two weeks each month and a winery operator the rest of the time. While Captain Bill is maneuvering ships, the Lucas ladies, wife Ruth and daughters, Ruthie and Stephanie, manage the retail operation and host tour groups, and winemaker Steve DiFrancesco tends to the wine production.

The stately Lucas home and winery is the center of visitor activity and special summer wine and food events. When you purchase a case of Lucas wine you automatically become a member of their Wine Club, complete with special discounts, and you are invited to the Annual Club Party (the highlight of the season).

Captain Bill would like to retire to the comforts of his country estate and just make wine, but recent additions and improvements have necessitated an additional couple of years of earning that "saltwater money" to help pay the bills.

Pork Meatballs with Caramelized Sweet & Sour Sauce
A Different Pesto

MC GREGOR VINEYARD
5503 Dutch St.
(East side of Keuka Lake, off Rte. 54)
Dundee, NY 14837
(607) 292-3999

Since Bob McGregor opened his winery in 1980, he has decided to take an alternate path in marketing his winery.

The McGregor family is continually looking for new ways to improve, expand and enhance their product line while pursuing the winery's interest in showcasing wine with food. And how fortunate for us!

They already sponsor a highly successful "Strawberries and Champagne" event each June plus a "Spring Open House," a "Raspberries and Chocolate" promotion in July and produce a nouveau style wine so they can have an annual "Nouveau Party" in November.

The McGregor tasting room is a fun place to visit with its variety of unusual gift items, an excellent selection of well-made wines and a beautiful view of Keuka Lake. Picnic tables are available both outside and on the covered porch and the hospitality is plentiful.

Cheddar Wine Straws
Cheesy Wine Mold
Gruyere Stuffed Mushrooms
Mushroom Pastry
Keuka Lake Wine Cooler
Chocolate Raspberry Surprise
Late Harvest Gewürztraminer Cake
Barbecue Fish-Keuka Lake Style
Tarragon Wine Stuffing

MEIER'S WINE CELLARS
6955 Plainfield Pike
Silverton, OH 45236
(513) 891-2900

Meier's, Ohio's oldest and largest winery, has been making wine for more than 100 years. Many of Meier's premium wines have been selected as award-winners at prestigious competitions both nationally and internationally.

Although the actual Meier's Tasting Room and Wine Shop is near Cincinnati and outside of the Great Lakes Region, it is part of the Firelands Cooperative Winery in Sandusky and much of their fruit comes from the area.

Meier's is also sponsor of a number of cooking classes at the winery featuring its popular corporate chef Tom Johnson. Meier's cooking classes consist of hands-on participation and are limited to 20 people. Following a detailed run-through of the recipes, including a specific demonstration by Chef Johnson, the class is divided into teams, each preparing a designated recipe. The best part comes at the end of the class when the students and instructor move from the kitchen to the dining table and partake of the food which they created.

Tiramisu
Coq au Vin Longworth
Lentil-Leek Soup with Fresh Ginger and Sherry

MON AMI RESTAURANT & WINERY
3845 East Wine Cellar Rd.
Port Clinton, OH 43452
(419) 797-4445
(800) 777-4266

Most winery/restaurant combinations develop their food service operation around the success of the winery trade. At Mon Ami, the emphasis is definitely on food. The winery is part of the Firelands Wine Cooperative which serves as the central processing plant for the 26 varieties of wine under the Mon Ami label. The restaurant is an extension of the Zappone family whose culinary history began with Grandma Zappone making pasta dishes above the family grocery store some 80 years ago.

The Mon Ami winery was constructed in 1872 of local native materials. This building now houses the restaurant, sales and gift shop on the main floor, with banquet and private party facilities on the second floor, and a sparkling wine cellar in the basement.

From May through September, the Mon Ami is one of the busiest places in the area. From "Jazz Outdoors" to live entertainment in the Chalet Lounge indoors, to various barbecues and an inviting dining room menu, the Mon Ami lives up to its cordial name; "My Friend."

Red Onion Tartar Sauce
Goujonnetes of Lake Erie Walleye
Pan-Grilled Scampi in Chardonnay Sauce

NORTHLAND WINERY
4018 Middle Ridge Rd
Perry, OH 44081
(216) 259-2652

Some of the best career advice to give young people is "to find something you like to do, learn all you can about it and stick with it." While researching a senior high school project about winemaking, Richard Kovacic did just that. Fifteen years later, Kovacic is more knowledgeable about winemaking, still young and with his wife Catherine, has opened a small winery.

Northland Vineyards patterns itself after wineries the Kovacics have visited in Canada on numerous occasions. "We really love the Ontario wine region and we like how easy it is to go from one winery to another while enjoying the area at the same time. We have a number of wineries near us and we'd like to encourage that same type of activity, " explains Catherine, who presides over the business aspect of the couple's venture.

"I'm really proud of what Richard has accomplished," Catherine says enthusiastically, "this is all he has ever done. It's his life. We're not a big farm, we're just simple people making wine."
Cream of Brie Soup

OLD FIREHOUSE WINERY
5499 Lake Rd., Box 310
Geneva-on-the-Lake, OH 44041
(216) 466-9300

A 1924 Dodge Firetruck, the city's original firebarn, a hospitality room full of nostalgic fire-fighting paraphernalia and the serene beauty of the Lake Erie shoreline are all features of this most unique winery. Located right in the heart of the resort town of Geneva-on-the-Lake, the Old Firehouse Winery sits on the Lake Erie shore and offers magnificent summer sunsets and fantastic winter landscapes. On weekends during the summer tourist season, however, "the joint starts jumpin'!" From live entertainment, to an annual Celtic Fest, to clambakes and food extravaganzas, the fun doesn't stop at this popular gathering spot.

Only a small amount of Old Firehouse wine is actually produced on the premises (under 2,000 gallons), but they are nicely made, refreshing and add to the pleasure of a leisurely afternoon or casual evening on The Old Firehouse outdoor deck and gazebo.
Zabaglione
Bourdelaise Sauce
Baked Beans in Cider

PETERSON AND SONS WINERY
9375 East P Ave.
Kalamazoo, MI 49001-9762
(616) 626-9755

Duane, Tony and Todd Peterson's label is called "Naturally Old Fashioned Wines" and boasts of its use of "No Chemicals or Sulfites" added to the production of their wine. This claim, plus the emphasis on producing unusual fruit wines such as Rhubarb/Cherry, Red and Black Raspberry, Cranberry/Raspberry and Wild Elderberry, has put Peterson and Sons Winery in a unique market niche.

Peterson explains, "With our style of wine and working with small fifty-five gallon batches, we just felt it wasn't necessary to use chemicals. I'm not sure why, but everything seems to work and there are more and more new customers that agree with our philosophy and old-fashioned way of making wine. I consider our method of winemaking an art form and a gift...I just don't question the results."

Natural Fruit Champagne Cocktails
Raspberry Lovers' Super Dessert

REIF ESTATE WINERY
   15608 Niagara Parkway, R.R. 1
   Niagara-on-the-Lake, Ontario L0S 1J0
   (905) 468-7738

After thirteen generations of winemakers with 300 years of experience, one would think that a winemaking family with such an ancestry would be well set in their ways. In the case of Germany's Reif family, tradition is limited to quality. Beyond that there are no boundaries for expansion and experimentation.

In the 1960's and 70's, Reif family members began scouring the world for a location to build and develop another winery. They came to the Niagara Peninsula and decided this was the area for the family to invest in expansion. When the Reif family purchased their vineyard land, it included a spectacular mansion (circa 1880) on the scenic Niagara River Parkway. This palatial residence, which displays the opulence and grandiose style typical of the Victorian era, has been converted into a magnificent bed & breakfast and has been aptly named "The Grand Victorian." The structure is so dominating that it may occupy your attention as you pass by the entrance next door to the converted stables that now house the Reif winery and tasting room.

Sautéed Mushrooms on Toasted Hearts
Riesling Cake
Barbecued Loin Pork Chops
Klauses Lamb in Chardonnay
Turkey Breast in Vidal Cream Sauce
Shrimp and Scallop Chowder from the Microwave

ST JULIAN WINE COMPANY
   716 S. Kalamazoo St.
   Paw Paw, MI 49079
   (616) 657-5568

Modern winemaking throughout the world is deeply embedded in family traditions. Some of those family histories expand to the "New World" and include the Great Lakes Region. One such family of winemakers are the Meconi's who record five generations of winemaking in Italy. The sixth generation descendant, Mariano Meconi, decided to practice his trade across the ocean and created what is now known as the St. Julian Wine Company. Two more Meconi generations have since evolved and have combined to create the largest winery in Michigan with seven tasting rooms in major tourist areas around the state.

The winery location in Paw Paw also offers a very attractive and popular Italian-style cafe or *trattoria*. Besides offering sandwiches, pizza and light entrees, *Apollo's* houses an enchanting toy museum for young and old alike.

St. Julian, the patron saint of Falaria, Italy, birthplace of the Meconi family, has looked favorably upon its descendants and has blessed the food and wine-loving public with the delicious fruits of their efforts.

Light and Fresh Sangria
Double Chocolate Cheesecake with Raspberry Glaze
Red Wine Raspberry Sorbet
Herbed Potatoes
Puffed Polo
Great White Garlic Soup
Solera Mushroom Soup
Spicy Shrimp Salad

SWEDISH HILL VINEYARDS & WINERY
4565 Route 414
Romulus, NY 14541
(315) 549-8326

A trip to the Swedish Hill Winery is an enjoyable experience. The scenic landscape is accented with beautiful farmland and entering the tasting room is worth the visit in itself. A spacious retail room is jam-packed with winery antiques and paraphernalia as well as wine-related gift items of every type. Gift baskets are a specialty of the winery and just about every size, shape and description of basket and wine "goodies" and "trinkets" are offered.

There is a special event every month at the winery, so you may want to call ahead to make plans. Even if you just casually stop in, put on your shopping shoes, then finish the afternoon on the deck with a glass of wine, some light food and a wonderful country view. What better things are there in life?

Spicy Swenska Chicken

TABOR HILL WINERY AND RESTAURANT
185 Mt. Tabor Road
Buchanan, MI 49107
(800) 283-3363

Imagine yourself driving through the countryside of Southwest Michigan on what appears to be a road to nowhere surrounded by rolling hills and fragrant vineyards. Then imagine coming upon a quaint and intimate little winery and restaurant nestled high on a hill overlooking vineyards and the Lake Michigan dunes beyond. That is exactly what you will see, when you find Tabor Hill, which is correctly nicknamed "The Hidden Jewel."

Tabor Hill exemplifies the philosophy that wine is a "food beverage" and consequently the winemakers have created wines to accompany foods that will enhance any dining occasion. With your first dining experience at Tabor Hill, it becomes apparent why so many people continue to make the effort to travel to this isolated location for lunch or dinner.

With its picturesque view overlooking the countryside amidst the fluttering and feeding of colorful finches, this restaurant is definitely a credit to Tabor Hill in offering some of the best agriculture the Great Lakes has to offer in both food and wine.

Crayfish Soup

VON STIEHL WINERY
115 Navarino Street
Algoma, WI 54201
(414) 487-5208

Cherry wine is king on the Door County Peninsula and the von Stiehl Winery has made the most of a good thing by pleasing customers and winning awards for their peninsula cherry wine since 1964. The von Stiehl Winery is the oldest continuous winery in the state of Wisconsin and is situated in a former brewery built in 1868 in the quaint little town of Algoma just a thirty minute drive east of Green Bay.

In the early years of the winery, Charles Stiehl, a medical doctor, hand-wrapped his precious bottles of cherry and apple wine with protective gauze and encased it with a plaster of paris mixture. This patented process was created to protect the wine from sunlight and changing temperatures. The "bottle cast" is still used on a limited number of bottles of the winery's signature cherry wine.

Cherry Nut Loaf Quick Bread
Ham Steak with Class
Wine & Wild Rice Bake

WAGNER VINEYARDS
9322 Route 414
Lodi, NY 14860
(607) 582-6450

As a lifelong resident and a grape grower for over forty years, Bill Wagner is considered a modern-era pioneer and visionary for the Finger Lakes farm wineries. Bill began building his famous, self-designed octagon-shaped winery in 1975. Ever since then, Wagner has continually led the way for an onrush of new wineries which has consequently meant a steady stream of tourists in the Finger Lakes region. Most recently Wagner has taken on another project with the expansion of his Ginny Lee Cafe next door. What started out as a tent-covered deck serving sandwiches is now a full-fledged restaurant tending to guests for lunch or brunch indoors or *al fresco* on the deck overlooking a beautiful view of Seneca Lake. The Ginny Lee has also become the most desirable spot for a romantic wedding reception.

Ravat Blanc Mousse

WARNER VINEYARDS
706 S. Kalamazoo St.
Paw Paw, MI 49079
(616) 657-3165

Three generations of Warner's have overseen this Michigan winemaking firm since its inception in 1938 as an adjunct to the family banking, farm-supply and farming businesses. Situated on the riverbank in downtown Paw Paw, the heart of Michigan's wine country, Warner has transposed the village's old water-works building into the winery's visitors' center. This state-designated historical structure, built in 1898, is unique with its interesting architecture of an exaggerated roof line and tall, solitary chimney. Inside this unusual facade is the visitors' tasting room which also features a re-creation display of European Champagne Caves. Warner specializes in *méthode champenoise* sparkling wines which are carefully nurtured toward a second fermentation process within each bottle. The trapped gases of this fermentation are what give the wine its bubbles.

Adjacent to the tasting-room building is an old 1914 Grand Trunk Railroad passenger rail car that serves as a popular gift shop and curiosity attraction.

Wine Cheese Spread
Strawberry or Peach Refresher
Sweet and Sour Rabbit
Winemaker's Spanish Rice
Vintner's Chicken
Liebestrauben Glazed Carrots

Late Addition:
MICHIGAN VINTNER WINE CO.
  4014 Bell Ave NE
  Grand Rapids, MI 49505
  (616) 363-9637

Like most "micro-wineries," Michigan Vintner started as a hobby and quickly got out of control. Today, this eleven-barrel winery produces only about 600 gallons annually at the winery facilities of Fenn Valley Vineyards. Consequently, at the moment, Michigan Vintner does not have its own building for touring and tasting. The winemaking partners do, however, have an enormous love and desire for both wine and food . . . and that we can share with them.

Veal Shanks Great Lakes Style
Chicken Broth
Thunder and Lightning

Recipe Index

Great Lakes Contributing Wineries